Implementing SAP® Customer Competence Center

SAP® Essentials

Expert SAP knowledge for your day-to-day work

Whether you wish to expand your SAP knowledge, deepen it, or master a use case, SAP Essentials provide you with targeted expert knowledge that helps support you in your day-to-day work. To the point, detailed, and ready to use.

SAP PRESS is a joint initiative of SAP and Galileo Press. The know-how offered by SAP specialists combined with the expertise of the Galileo Press publishing house offers the reader expert books in the field. SAP PRESS features first-hand information and expert advice, and provides useful skills for professional decision-making.

SAP PRESS offers a variety of books on technical and business related topics for the SAP user. For further information, please visit our website: *www.sap-press.com.*

Raju, Wallacher
B2B Integration Using SAP NetWeaver PI
2008, 450 pp., ISBN 978-1-59229-163-2

Banner, Gürsoy, Klein
Mastering SAP NetWeaver XI — Programming
2007, 107 pp., ISBN 978-1-59229-140-3

Heilig, Karch, Böttcher, Mutzig, Weber, Pfennig
SAP NetWeaver: The Official Guide
2008, 489 pp., ISBN 978-1-59229-193-9

Karch, Heilig
SAP NetWeaver Roadmap
2005, 305 pp., ISBN 978-1-59229-041-3

Boris Otto, Jörg Wolter

Implementing SAP® Customer Competence Center

Galileo Press

Bonn • Boston

ISBN 978-1-59229-258-5

© 2009 by Galileo Press Inc., Boston (MA)
1st Edition 2009

German Edition first published 2008 by Galileo Press, Bonn, Germany

Galileo Press is named after the Italian physicist, mathematician and philosopher Galileo Galilei (1564–1642). He is known as one of the founders of modern science and an advocate of our contemporary, heliocentric worldview. His words *Eppur si muove* (And yet it moves) have become legendary. The Galileo Press logo depicts Jupiter orbited by the four Galilean moons, which were discovered by Galileo in 1610.

Editor Mirja Werner
English Translation Editor Jon Franke
Translation Lemoine International, Inc., Salt Lake City UT
Copyeditor Julie McNamee
Cover Design Jill Winitzer
Photo Credit Fotolia/Oliver Rüttimann
Production Editor Kelly O'Callaghan
Layout Design Vera Brauner
Typesetting Publishers' Design and Production Services, Inc.
Printed and bound in Canada

Contents

Preface

Global market presence, customer-specific requirements, and the increasing significance of service are forcing enterprises to continuously develop and adapt their business models. Services are increasingly performed in networks, and value structures are changing.

Business success depends more and more on the contribution of information technology (IT). In many enterprises, IT no longer assumes a sole support function but forms an integral part of the business processes. The deep integration of processes and the availability of real-time information in core processes are only possible with a powerful IT architecture.

Due to this close connection with the core business, the availability of IT support assumes a business-critical role today. IT needs to be reliable — 365 days, 24/7, worldwide — in a lot of enterprises. This requires the IT processes and the support processes and organization to be consistently oriented toward the business processes, as well as an efficient management of the IT services.

Since the mid-1990s, enterprises have organized their support with SAP-focused business solutions in SAP Customer Competence Center (SAP CCC). SAP CCC acts as a partner for the user departments in enterprises and a facilitator for the operational SAP business. Thanks to the great commitment of SAP customers and partners, the number of SAP CCCs has grown significantly, and the concept has turned into a real success story.

The need to link business process knowledge and SAP solutions expertise has continuously increased in the past years. Against this background, you must adapt the support organization to get the most out of the established SAP solutions and new technologies, such as the Business Process Platform, the SAP NetWeaver platform, enterprise service-oriented architecture (enterprise SOA), or SAP Solution Manager. Only in this case does IT act as the driving force for business innovations and enable a continuous improvement of the business processes. This also requires an adaptation and, in some cases, a reorganization of SAP CCC in the enterprise, in short, a "next generation CCC." It is essential for SAP to provide the best possible support and assistance to customers in this process. Thanks to its holistic view and real-world recommendations, this SAP Press Essentials Guide represents a valuable contribution.

I hope that you'll enjoy reading the book and wish you all the best for the implementation of SAP CCC.

Gerhard Oswald
Member of the Board, SAP AG

1 Introduction

SAP Customer Competence Center (SAP CCC) bundles all competencies regarding SAP solutions in an enterprise and functions as a link between the different organizational units within the enterprise (user departments, IT organization) and external partners (SAP, service providers).

1.1 Goals of this Book

The significance of SAP solutions continuously grows for core business processes in enterprises. This involves an increase of requirements for reliability, availability, performance, and security of the application operation and support organization.

To meet these requirements and actively manage complexity, risk, and cost, SAP CCCs need to be consistently improved in enterprises.

The goal of this book is to indicate the fields of activity that are necessary for this consistent improvement, to derive concrete measures for the implementation, and to refer to new supporting SAP services. This includes revised reference processes, enhanced standard procedures, and improved support tools.

1.2 Target Group

This book addresses decision makers and line managers in enterprises that are responsible for the setup, development, and operation of SAP solutions, for example, chief information officers (CIOs), IT managers, business area managers, user department managers, process managers, program managers, IT strategists, and SAP CCC managers. This book is also interesting for those involved in an SAP program or the SAP operating organization in an enterprise.

This book doesn't require product-specific or technical SAP knowledge. However, it helps if you have knowledge about basic concepts of the operation of SAP solutions.

1.3   Structure of the Book

Chapter 2 introduces SAP CCC, identifies fields of activity, and provides an overview of the success factors for setup and operation.

An efficiently and effectively working support organization requires a superordinate SAP CCC strategy, whose components and development are described in **Chapter 3**.

The integration of SAP CCC with the enterprise organization and the implementation of the appropriate strategy require a suitable tool, that is, a practical governance model. This model names the basic functions of SAP CCC, identifies the roles and committee structures involved, and defines the responsibilities. **Chapter 4** introduces the corresponding best practices and recommends procedures for the implementation.

Chapter 5 describes how SAP CCC additionally specifies the process organization on the basis of the de-facto standard for the IT service management, the IT Infrastructure Library (ITIL), and its enhancement by SAP in the form of SAP IT Service & Application Management.

Based on this, **Chapter 6** focuses on the IT support of SAP CCC. In this context, SAP Solution Manager provides numerous new scenarios that are outlined in an overview and represented with a roadmap for the SAP Solution Manager implementation.

Chapter 7 discusses future requirements for the qualification of the SAP CCC employees and introduces approaches for qualification measures.

To determine the starting point for improvements, **Chapter 8** describes an SAP CCC maturity model. **Chapter 9** deals with the service portfolio that SAP offers to support enterprises in setting up or further developing their SAP CCC.

Finally, **Chapter 10** provides an outlook on current and future trends — for example, enterprise SOA, Expertise on Demand — and discusses their relevance for the support organization.

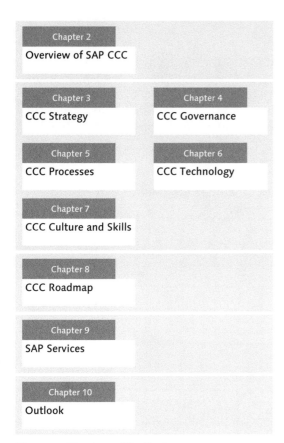

Figure 1.1 Structure of the Book

Figure 1.1 shows an overview of the book's structure. Chapters 3 to 7 are combined in one area because they include the fields of modeling that you must consider when setting up SAP CCC. Chapters 8 and 9, however, deal with the supporting instruments and tools.

1.4 Terminology Used

The content of this book is based on internationally recognized standards, such as the IT Infrastructure Library (ITIL), and thus also uses the terminology of these standards.

1.5   Acknowledgements

Without great support, careful preparations, and constructive criticism, we wouldn't have been able to write this book. We would like to thank the following persons and organizations for their support:

- DSAG (German-Speaking SAP User Group) for its support in surveys
- SAP CCC Community, particularly Liane Will, Sigrid Hagemann, Simon Bertels, and Dirk Baudisch for the technical feedback
- Frank Moersch and Klaus Hertweck for editing the graphics in the illustrations
- Mirja Werner, Jon Franke, and Julie McNamee for the commitment at SAP Press
- Our families for their understanding

Boris Otto and Jörg Wolter

2 An Overview of SAP CCC

SAP Customer Competence Center (SAP CCC) is an organizational unit of the customer enterprise that bundles the SAP competences. Its basic purposes are to consolidate the SAP resources in an enterprise and function as a link between the user department and IT organization.

This chapter first provides an overview of the driving force for the integration of SAP CCC as well as its main tasks. It then describes the fields of activity that are relevant for designing SAP CCC. Finally, the chapter identifies the success factors and introduces the results of a current survey of the priorities of CCC managers.

2.1 Driving Forces

SAP CCC basically serves to continuously improve the support of business processes with SAP solutions by enabling you to increase the effectiveness and efficiency of business processes (see Figure 2.1).

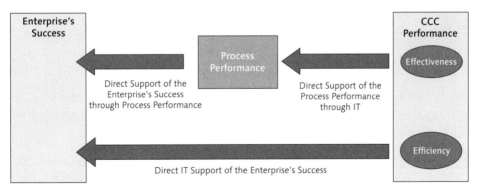

Figure 2.1 Driving Forces

The *effectiveness* of SAP CCC is, among other things, indicated by the following effects:

▶ You can more easily fulfill the business requirements and cover the business processes by using SAP solutions.

▶ The objectives of the enterprise are supported, for example, reducing the process costs and lead times.

▶ The adaptability and flexibility of the IT operation increase with respect to changing requirements of the user departments.

▶ Innovative solutions are developed by means of innovative technologies, such as Radio Frequency Identification (RFID).

▶ The usage rate of SAP solutions grows in the enterprise.

SAP CCC increases the *efficiency* of the enterprise by:

▶ Improving the investment control, for example, by using an optimized SAP release strategy and the SAP Resource and Portfolio Management (SAP RPM) solution for the IT project portfolio management

▶ Promoting the standardization and harmonization of the IT landscape

▶ Improving the cost management of IT services, for example, by outsourcing development activities

▶ Professionalizing the SAP project management, for example, by using SAP roadmaps

▶ Reducing the dependency on external consultants, for example, by using best-practices for implementation and operation

2.2   Tasks

Due to the customer-specific design of SAP CCC, it has a varying range of tasks. However, most of the support organizations have the same focus when establishing SAP CCC:

▶ Providing a central point of contact for SAP solutions within and outside the customer organization

▶ Mapping an end-to-end solution support for holistic support and monitoring of business processes

▶ Consulting for, implementing, operating, and optimizing SAP solutions

▶ Linking the user departments with the operational SAP business

The responsibility for the support of efficient implementations and permanent development, maintenance, and quality assurance of SAP solutions, for example, further specify these tasks.

As an interface to SAP, SAP CCC also coordinates the collaboration with SAP employees from the support, consulting, sales, training, and development departments. This collaboration includes operational tasks, such as problem handling and solving, as well as an early knowledge transfer regarding new solutions.

Many enterprises have also contracted for SAP CCC setups because you require a certification by SAP to grant discounts for the maintenance costs. This certification is linked to the integration of specific SAP CCC basic functions.

2.3 Fields of Activity

From the experience with numerous customer projects, SAP has derived five basic fields of activity that are considered essential and, in this sense, as best practices for setting up SAP CCC (see Figure 2.2).

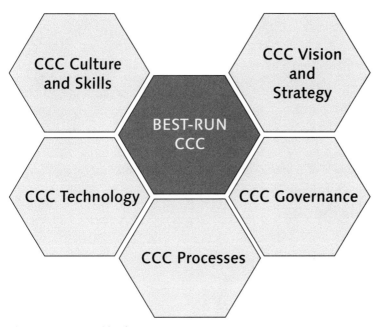

Figure 2.2 CCC Fields of Activity

2.3.1 CCC Strategy

The CCC strategy is responsible for the integration of SAP CCC with the IT strategy and thus indirectly with the business strategy. It contains a strategic model, including a mission statement of the major objectives, and also provides information on the management system and the benefit contribution of SAP CCC and the business objectives.

2.3.2 CCC Governance

SAP CCC is not isolated from the rest of the organization. Instead, it is linked to numerous other organizational units and external actors. A *governance model* specifies which tasks and functions are relevant for these relationships, which roles and committees they involve, and how freedom of decision and responsibilities are defined.

2.3.3 CCC Processes

Like the organizational embedding, the *process organization* also lays the foundation for the operational operation of SAP CCC. You must design the processes in a way that the CCC resources can be used as effectively and efficiently as possible. Consequently, the SAP recommendations for the SAP CCC processes are based on established standards, such as ITIL, and best practices, such as *SAP Standards for Solution Operations*.

2.3.4 CCC Technology

The CCC processes achieve only a high efficiency if you use the appropriate tools. The *SAP Solution Manager* provides a central technology for the user operation.

2.3.5 CCC Culture and Skills

The requirements for the qualification of the SAP CCC employees are changing. In the future, you will require comprehensive business process expertise and knowledge about new technologies. Among other things, you also need a role-based qualification strategy for these changed requirements.

2.4   Success Factors

You can derive numerous central success factors by analyzing customer projects:

▶ The management from the user department and IT organization supports the setup and further development of SAP CCC.

▶ The user departments and IT in the enterprise are closely linked.

▶ The user department and IT organization are aware of a comprehensive service management. This is indicated, for example, by considering the IT an organizational unit that creates added value and doesn't only incur costs.

▶ A comprehensive innovation management is integrated.

▶ The necessary resources are available for the CCC transformation process in the user department and IT organization.

2.5   Real-Life Priorities

The diversity of SAP CCC tasks is reflected in the results of a survey among 200 CCC managers. The survey intended to identify the most important subject areas in real-world CCC implementations (see Figure 2.3).

Implementation of Enterprise-Strategic Projects	**1**	1.78
Development of Business Process Knowledge in CCC Organization	**2**	1.91
Improvement of CCC Service Quality	**3**	1.97
Recruitment, Training, and Retention of CCC Personnel	**4**	2.09
Improvement of CCC Project Management	**5**	2.26
Indication of Value Contribution of CCC Organization	**6**	2.31
Establishment of CCC Governance	**7**	2.53
Flexibility of Technological Infrastructure (e.g., Enterprise SOA)	**8**	2.60
Usage of Measurement and Leading Values in CCC Organization	**9**	2.61

Figure 2.3   CCC Priorities (1 = Top Priority to 5 = No Priority) Source: DSAG/SAP 2007

According to this survey, the three most important subject areas are the following:

▶ **Implementation of enterprise-strategic projects**
More than 85% of all participants consider the support of enterprise-strategic projects as a high or the highest priority of the CCC organization.

▶ **Improvement of the CCC service quality**
To fulfill the increased requirements of the business areas for the CCC organization, the organization must provide reliable services.

▶ **Development of business process knowledge in the CCC organization**
Eight out of ten participants specify that the development of knowledge in technical issues is absolutely necessary.

These three topics show that today an SAP CCC cannot merely be restricted to working according to the rules. Moreover, it is supposed to actively design and promote transformation processes in an enterprise on the basis of SAP solutions.

This requires an integrated management of the CCC organization that comprises all fields of activity that are mentioned in Section 2.3.

This book uses real-world experience to support you in implementing SAP CCC successfully.

3 Developing SAP CCC Strategies

Setting up SAP CCC becomes a task with strategic dimensions due to the enterprise-wide scope of SAP solutions and their use for the support of core business processes.

This chapter outlines how you can design an SAP CCC strategy, ensure a smooth integration with the business and IT strategy of your enterprise, set up a management system, and develop a suitable CCC roadmap.

3.1 Motivation

Setting up SAP CCC is always linked with the far-reaching decision to implement SAP as the standard software in your enterprise. In this context, different objectives are pursued; for example, SAP solutions enable the integrated and continuous support of business processes across enterprise and business areas. Vendors as well as customers can be integrated with the process chains here. This integration reduces the gaps in the business processes, counteracts redundant data maintenance, and decreases the process lead times. Employees are provided with business information according to their respective roles.

Due to this importance for the enterprise and to ensure a holistic management of the SAP solutions, you require a superordinate CCC strategy. Such a strategy enables you to ideally exploit the benefits of SAP CCC:

- Fast adaptability to continuously changing business requirements
- Immediate availability of expertise for business processes and the corresponding SAP solution
- Long-term plannability and controllability of the strategic business process architecture
- Cross-departmental cost control for the entire lifecycle of the SAP solutions
- Reduced IT costs through continuous optimization of the IT infrastructure

- Fewer problems and escalation events in the IT operation

- Accelerated communication channels between SAP and the customer enterprise

A sustained CCC strategy includes a *model* and a *mission statement*. It comprises strategic targets and statements about how these targets are achieved and how the degree of target achievement is measured. A CCC strategy should meet the following requirements:

- Integration of the CCC strategy with the business and IT strategy

- Clear alignment of the CCC strategy with the requirements of the departments and the business objectives of the enterprise

- Long-term planning horizon

The following sections include examples of CCC strategies of some enterprises:

- "We create a permanent center of SAP specialist competence within the group to support the implementation, enhancement, and operation of the shared business processes and systems."

- "We want to offer support at the business level to provide precise information in a timely manner at lowest possible costs."

- "SAP CCC is supposed to function as an internal service provider to support and develop SAP activities in order to directly contribute to the successful business processing."

3.2   Mission Statement and Vision

A *mission statement* for SAP CCC defines the long-term orientation, concepts, and ideals of the CCC organization. Examples of such statements include the following:

- "There is no better way to run SAP."

- "We want to support our business areas to achieve clear, sustained, and considerable business benefits through the use of SAP solutions and to create an excellent organization that can attract, develop, and inspire extraordinary people to retain them for the enterprise."

▶ "Our SAP CCC creates value-oriented SAP solutions to support innovation, growth, and profitability."

▶ "Accelerate the use of SAP to support the business strategy — growth and enhancement in value."

The mission statement is further detailed in a *strategic vision* for SAP CCC. This model specifies the overall image and creates a common understanding of how the mission statement is to be implemented.

Figure 3.1 illustrates the different dimensions of such a strategic vision based on a customer example. The guidelines for the employees and their working method, the quality of the CCC services, and the used CCC tools are predefined. These criteria can be used to subsequently measure the management and employees. In this example, the dimensions of the CCC strategy orient toward the SAP slogan "The best-run businesses run SAP" and consequently specify the mission statement to make a contribution so that the enterprise is among the best of its industry segment.

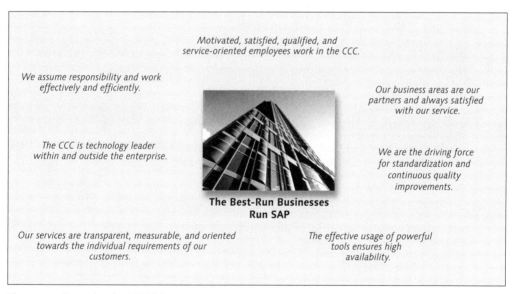

Motivated, satisfied, qualified, and service-oriented employees work in the CCC.

We assume responsibility and work effectively and efficiently.

Our business areas are our partners and always satisfied with our service.

The CCC is technology leader within and outside the enterprise.

We are the driving force for standardization and continuous quality improvements.

The Best-Run Businesses Run SAP

Our services are transparent, measurable, and oriented towards the individual requirements of our customers.

The effective usage of powerful tools ensures high availability.

Figure 3.1 Example of a CCC Vision

Real-world experience shows that the development of a mission statement and strategic model results in several decisive benefits:

► Holistic clarification of the course of action of each employee

► Promotion of shared values among the CCC employees

► Focus of the organization on shared targets, particularly during the developing stage and in critical situations

· Sustained motivation of SAP CCC's management and employees

► Balance of competing and contradictory interests of the various stakeholders

► Superordinate value system for decision-making support

During the development of the mission statement and the strategic vision, you should include all stakeholders — and particularly the employees — in the strategy development process. This increases the acceptance and stability of a strategy.

3.3 Derivation from Business and IT Strategy

Within an enterprise, IT is not just used as an end in itself but helps to achieve the business targets. As a result, the IT strategy must be aligned with the business strategy to measure the value proposition of IT.

The strategy for SAP CCC provides a measurable specification of the IT strategy for that part of the IT organization that is responsible for the SAP solution landscape within the enterprise. Current trends, existing risks, and future options directly influence the modeling of the CCC strategy. The influencing factors arise from the CCC environment, that is, technological innovations (e.g., enterprise SOA and Dynamic Global Positioning System, DGPS), organizational basic conditions of the enterprise (e.g., restructurings), changed customer requirements, and increased service awareness.

Additionally, the CCC strategy considers the initial situation so that you can measure and compare the effects of strategic measures. To record the initial situation, SAP offers *assessments* that determine the core competencies of SAP CCC and implement an analysis of strengths and weaknesses, for example.

Moreover, the strategy comprises statements about the instruments used for the implementation. These include widely accepted standards of the IT service management, such as ITIL and *Control Objectives for Information and Related Technology*

(CobiT). CobiT provides the framework for the processes and their control modules for the IT infrastructure. (For more information refer to [Schöler 07].)

The value of a CCC strategy directly depends on the targets' quality that is to be achieved. Therefore, the SMART principle applies to the strategic target system of SAP CCC: The targets are to be **S**pecific, **M**easurable, **A**chievable, **R**ealistic, and **T**imely.

The target system can then be transferred to a measure system via *key performance indicators* (KPI). An example of such a KPI is the ratio of costs for operating applications and systems and the total IT costs. The strategy of SAP CCC could then include the strategic target to reduce the operating cost KPI from 67% to 65%, for example.

Figure 3.2 illustrates the measure system of a practical example in the dimensions of a *balanced scorecard* (BSC) [Kaplan 97].

Financial Perspective		Process Perspective	
IT Costs/Turnover	< 1.9%	Process Maturity	> 3.2
IT Investments/Turnover	< 0.7%	Unplanned RFCs	< 10%
IT Operating Costs	< 65%	Capacity Load Utilization	> 80%
...	...	...	...
Customer Perspective		Innovation Perspective	
Customer Satisfaction	< 2.0	Employee Satisfaction	< 1.9
SLA Fulfillment	> 98%	Fluctation Rate	< 10%
Project Fulfillment	> 85%	Percentage of Internal/ External IT Employees	> 90%
...	...	...	...

Figure 3.2 Measure System – Customer Example

For this purpose, a detailed description of the KPIs is required for the dimensions, name, data determination, data preparation, and reporting, in the form of a KPI information sheet [Kütz 07]. The target system and the measure system constitute the *management system* of SAP CCC (see Section 3.5).

You can then derive measures from the strategic targets that will be used to achieve the targets. The strategic measures, in turn, can be bundled to form a CCC roadmap and can be aligned with the superordinate budget specifications and the IT project portfolios.

Figure 3.3 shows an overview of the entire strategy development process for SAP CCC and the corresponding implementation.

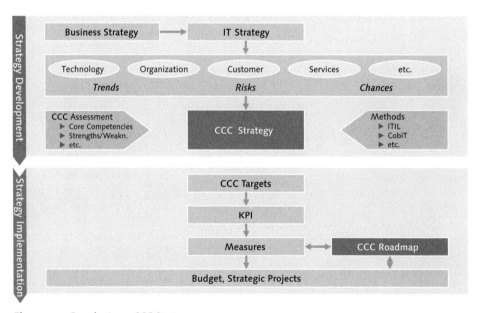

Figure 3.3 Developing a CCC Strategy

3.4 Strategy Components

The strategy for SAP CCC orients toward the IT strategy of an enterprise and develops it considering the SAP-specific issues of the IT organization. These SAP-specific issues derive from the components that are defined within the framework of an IT strategy. SAP identifies six basic components of an IT strategy (see Figure 3.4).

The strategy of SAP CCC must make statements taking into account these six key aspects as described in the following sections.

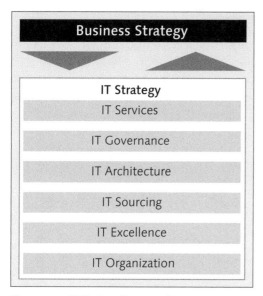

Figure 3.4 IT Strategy Framework

3.4.1 CCC Services

CCC services include the service to operate SAP solutions and to make them available to the users. This service is provided based on the *SAP IT Service & Application Management* (for more details refer to [Schöler05]), which is an enhancement of ITIL customized to the requirements of SAP solutions.

A typical example of a CCC service is the operation of a business application, such as SAP Customer Relationship Management (SAP CRM).

3.4.2 CCC Governance

CCC governance is the framework that determines the basic functions and decision areas in the context of SAP CCC, makes statements about the roles involved (from departments, IT organization, and external service providers), and assigns responsibilities. For example, the CCC governance must make statements about the standards to be used by the SAP application operation and who is involved in the decision about the enterprise-internal release planning for SAP solutions.

3.4.3 Architecture of the SAP Landscape

The central task of SAP CCC is to operate and further develop the SAP application landscape within the enterprise. For this purpose, the SAP architecture management must provide information, for example, which SAP solutions are used for functional and technical requirements, how the development plan of the SAP landscape must look, and how concepts, such as enterprise SOA, are to be implemented.

3.4.4 CCC Sourcing

The SAP *CCC sourcing* analyzes the SAP-related IT value chain within an enterprise and defines which CCC services are performed by the enterprise and which are bought on the market.

3.4.5 CCC Excellence

CCC excellence describes the professional implementation of the SAP CCC strategy by means of governance concepts as well as the management of CCC services in the lifecycle phases: *plan*, *build*, and *run*. SAP has compiled its experience from customer projects in the guides, *SAP IT Service & Application Management* [Schöler 2005], and SAP Standards for Solution Operations.

3.4.6 CCC Organization

Drawing on the future requirements of SAP solutions within the enterprise, measures must be planned and implemented for structuring and developing the CCC organization.

Figure 3.5 shows a customer example for the definition of the architecture strategy component for SAP CCC as well as for its alignment with the business strategy.

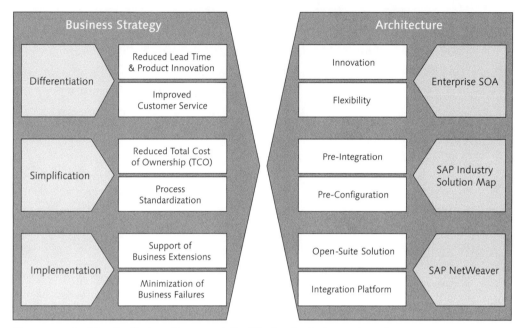

Figure 3.5 Deriving the Strategy Component "Architecture" – Customer Example

The strategic directions of the business strategy have been operationalized for the architecture of the SAP landscape so that they can be assigned to different effective directions of the SAP solutions used in the enterprise. For a concrete example, this means:

▶ **Enterprise Service-Oriented Architecture**
Service-oriented architectures are based on the concept of modularization and reusability of software components. This modularization promotes the simple and rapid support of new business processes, and the re-use of individual services in different processes.

▶ **SAP Industry Solution Map**
SAP is the industry-leading enterprise and provides an integration solution that is required to support your core and control processes. Therefore, the following prioritization applies to the IT support of your processes:

  ▶ Priority 1: SAP software

  ▶ Priority 2: Standard software

  ▶ Priority 3: Customer development based on SAP technologies

▶ **SAP NetWeaver**

SAP NetWeaver is the technology and infrastructure platform for most of the current and all future SAP developments and products. SAP NetWeaver enables the continuous reorganization of all products to the principles of a service-oriented architecture. The use of SAP NetWeaver therefore constitutes the basic module of the IT strategy.

3.5 Management System

After you analyze the business and IT strategy and define the strategic basic conditions for SAP CCC, you then define concrete targets. In real-world scenarios, the description of the target with a planning period of three to five years has proven itself.

Moreover, it's advisable to restrict the definition of targets to a manageable number. Three to five strategic targets constitute a reasonable range that allows for the focusing of resources to the most critical topics and also ensures that you don't get "bogged down" in a multitude of competing initiatives.

In addition, you must coordinate the KPIs and targets with all participants and ideally integrate them with the development of targets. Your motto should be "Direct involvement of those who will be affected by the project." Thereby, you achieve a high transparency both for how you measure the attainment of targets and the interpretation of KPI values.

Figure 3.6 illustrates an exemplary target matrix for SAP CCC. Because the target matrix is based on the dimensions of a BSC, it can be supported via tools such as *Outlooksoft*.

Strategic Targets			
	KPI	Specification	Measures
Increasing the business' success with continuous, proactive improvements of business activities and processes			
Increasing the efficiency of the CCC application provision with best practice transfers, standardization, and centralization			
...			
	KPI	Specification	Measures
Increasing the efficiency of the usage of applications by means of user trainings, requirement and innovation mgmt.			
...			
	KPI	Specification	Measures
Increasing flexibility by implementing service-oriented architectures (Enterprise SOA)			
...			
	KPI	Specification	Measures
Providing standardized processes, such as service support, service delivery, and so on			
...			

Value Contribution for the Enterprise

What are the Benefits of CCC?

Superior Operational Efficiency

Where Do We Have a Competitive Edge due to CCC?

Future Orientation

How Innovative is Our CCC?

User Orientation

What Does CCC Do for Our Internal and External Customers?

Figure 3.6 CCC Target Matrix

3.6   Roadmap

After you've aligned SAP CCC with the IT strategy and defined the strategic target system, you then define a *CCC roadmap* in the next step. A roadmap is enterprise-specific and depends on various influencing factors, such as the following:

▸ Targets of the CCC organization

▸ Current degree of maturity of CCC

▸ Planned functions

▸ Resources available

A roadmap therefore bundles several individual measures that all contribute to achieving the strategic CCC targets. Consequently, the roadmap must be created in close coordination with risk management, stakeholder management, and cost/benefit analysis.

3.7   Benefit Contribution

Enterprises that operate SAP CCC can significantly reduce the costs for the SAP system operation. For example, the costs for logged-on users are reduced by 13% and for *full-time users* by 17% [ASUG 07].

Additionally, SAP CCC allows for many further benefit potentials (see Figure 3.7).

Improvement of Business Processes	1	2.05
Provision of Central Financial and Management Information	2	2.11
Optimization of the Goods & Information Flow with Business Partners	3	2.38
Reduction of the Overhead Costs	4	2.52
Improvement of Customer Service and Customer Retention	5	2.53
Extension of Product Range with New Products and Services	6	2.90
Integration of Partner Network	7	2.94
Improvement of Sales Efficiency	8	3.06
Development of New Distribution Channels	9	3.47

Figure 3.7   Value Contributions of SAP CCC (1=Very High Contribution to 5=Very Low/No Contribution) Source: DSAG/SAP 2007

Besides the monetary benefit, CCC managers consider the improvement of process performance for business and specialist areas as the most valuable contribution of SAP CCC.

SAP has developed the *value assessment* method to identify and evaluate benefit potentials, as shown in Figure 3.8. This procedure compares the initial situation of the enterprise with best practices and benchmark data.

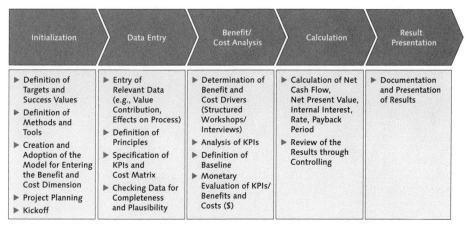

Initialization	Data Entry	Benefit/ Cost Analysis	Calculation	Result Presentation
▶ Definition of Targets and Success Values ▶ Definition of Methods and Tools ▶ Creation and Adoption of the Model for Entering the Benefit and Cost Dimension ▶ Project Planning ▶ Kickoff	▶ Entry of Relevant Data (e.g., Value Contribution, Effects on Process) ▶ Definition of Principles ▶ Specification of KPIs and Cost Matrix ▶ Checking Data for Completeness and Plausibility	▶ Determination of Benefit and Cost Drivers (Structured Workshops/ Interviews) ▶ Analysis of KPIs ▶ Definition of Baseline ▶ Monetary Evaluation of KPIs/ Benefits and Costs ($)	▶ Calculation of Net Cash Flow, Net Present Value, Internal Interest, Rate, Payback Period ▶ Review of the Results through Controlling	▶ Documentation and Presentation of Results

Figure 3.8 SAP Procedure Model Value Assessment

3.8 Summary

The establishment of SAP CCC has strategic dimensions in many enterprises because they support most business processes through SAP solutions (frequently on a global scale). A corresponding CCC strategy requires a vision and a mission statement, on the one hand, and the basic principles of various strategic components of CCC, such as governance and SAP architecture, on the other. It also includes strategic targets of CCC that are derived from the business and IT strategy and are controlled by a management system. A roadmap bundles all activities that are necessary to achieve the strategic targets. A continuous benefit analysis is required to make the contribution of CCC to the business targets transparent. For this purpose, the SAP value assessment approach helps you identify and evaluate the benefit potential.

4 Governance for SAP CCC

Governance for SAP CCC is intended to make the CCC strategy executable by integrating the strategic goals with the IT and the remaining enterprise organization.

4.1 Goals and Tasks

Establishing a governance model for SAP CCC serves the following purposes:

▶ Ensuring the continuous orientation of SAP CCC toward the objectives of the enterprise and business processes

▶ Optimizing the benefit contribution from the use of SAP solutions

▶ Ensuring the effective and efficient use of all CCC resources (employees, infrastructure, capital)

▶ Minimizing risks in the context of the SAP solution used

▶ Meeting the legal requirements (Sarbanes-Oxley Act, etc.)

From these objectives, you can derive the main tasks that you must perform to create a governance model:

▶ Identifying all task and decision areas that are required to implement the CCC strategy

▶ Identifying all involved actors (within and outside the IT organization)

▶ Setting up and staffing the necessary committees

▶ Mapping the tasks and responsibilities to roles

Basically, the governance model is responsible for solving the following issues:

▶ What is supposed to be defined?

▶ Who is involved?

▶ How are decisions made and responsibilities assigned?

The "What is supposed to be defined?" issue includes the following aspects (among others):

▶ Developing a strategy for SAP CCC

▶ Developing and establishing a management system

▶ Defining the CCC services

▶ Specifying standards for processes, services, and the architecture of the SAP application landscape

▶ Designing the IT supplier management

Each enterprise designs its own governance model. The existence of individual roles and the assignment of responsibilities depend on numerous influencing factors, for example, the size of the enterprise and the IT organization, the level of centralization, the geographical range, the qualification of the employees, and so on.

The governance model for SAP CCC thus provides the framework specified by the concrete design of the individual functions. The basic specifications include a description of the processes that SAP CCC executes (see Chapter 5).

4.2   Functions of SAP CCC

In accordance with ITIL, the main functions of SAP CCC can be divided into five areas: service strategy, service design, service transition, service operation, and continual service improvement.

4.2.1   SAP Service Strategy

The main task of the *SAP service strategy* is to encompass a strategic framework for SAP CCC and implement this framework in the CCC organization considering the business and IT strategy specifications. The SAP service strategy also monitors the implementation of the business case, which is subject to the use or introduction of SAP solutions, and defines the basic service portfolio.

4.2.2 SAP Service Design

To meet current and future business requirements, the *SAP service design* area defines the guidelines for the implementation and operation of SAP solutions. This includes, for example, architecture specifications and the design of ITIL service delivery processes.

4.2.3 SAP Service Transition

SAP service transition involves the further development of the infrastructure systems on which the SAP solutions run but also the application systems and the organizational processes for a high service quality. The spectrum ranges from importing simple patches, to carrying out comprehensive upgrade measures (e.g., for SAP R/3 to SAP ERP), and designing organizational change management and risk management.

4.2.4 SAP Service Operation

SAP service operation refers to the operation of SAP solutions. In addition to the IT service support processes, this encompasses further SAP tasks, such as root cause analysis, business process and interface monitoring, data volume management, job scheduling management, system administration, and system monitoring.

4.2.5 Continual Service Improvement

The continual optimization includes all areas of the ITIL service lifecycle. Practice has shown that the actual responsibilities and tasks of SAP CCC considerably differ for each enterprise. The descriptions in this book focus on the main functions of an SAP-focused IT organization that bundles its activities in SAP CCC.

4.3 Role Model

After analyzing all tasks, you identify and assign the corresponding roles. This step concerns the IT organization and the roles of the user departments. You must also consider the roles of external service providers and SAP.

Furthermore, you must differentiate between single roles and committees that contain various roles. Figure 4.1 shows sample roles that are involved in the SAP application operation.

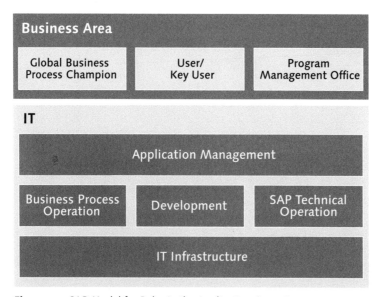

Figure 4.1 SAP Model for Roles in the Application Operation

This model, which is based on SAP best practices, considers the difference between roles in the user department and in the IT organization, and the general division of labor in the IT area.

A clear division of tasks lays the foundation for an effective and efficient operation of SAP. Dividing tasks is also a prerequisite for outsourcing task blocks of less strategic significance to external partners (see Section 4.6).

The mapping of roles to units in the user department and IT organization may also vary within the enterprise.

4.3.1 Roles Within the SAP Application Operation

The following list briefly describes the most important roles for the SAP application operation:

▶ The *users* are the main stakeholders in the user departments because they deploy the implemented SAP functions in their daily work. If questions or problems occur, they are supported by so-called *key users* that have a thorough knowledge of the SAP business applications.

▶ *Global business process champions* are responsible for designing and further developing the business processes in the business area and user departments. Consequently, they are the most critical customers of SAP CCC.

▶ The technical *program management* consolidates and prioritizes the requirements of the business areas and forwards these requirements to the CCC organization. The IT organization then ensures that the SAP services are available for the business areas.

▶ The *application manager* directly communicates with the business areas. He is particularly responsible for the implementation of the technical requirements and supports the users or key users. In this context, the application manager is supported by additional IT organizational units.

▶ The *business process operation* role is responsible for the operation and monitoring of the business applications, integration of the applications, and automation of jobs. Today, the respective roles can only be found in a few customer organizations; however, they assume a central role in the integration of the end-to-end business process concept and in the support organization.

▶ The *customer development* area implements technical requirements that are covered by the standard functions of the SAP solutions.

▶ The *technical operation for SAP solutions* area is responsible for the general system administration.

▶ The *IT infrastructure* ensures a safe and reliable operation of the network and data center components.

There are usually further specializations of these roles. Figure 4.2, for example, shows an example of the main roles in the development and operation of SAP solutions as well as their assignment to the model. See Appendix A for a detailed description of these roles.

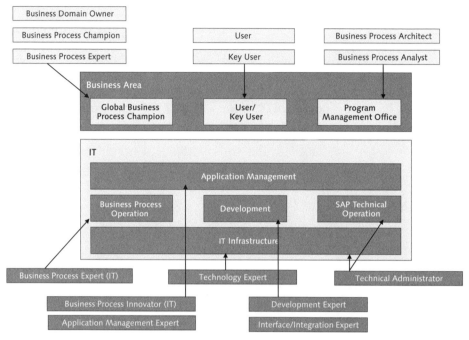

Figure 4.2 Interface Expert and Integration Expert Roles of Development

You can further specify these roles. For example, there are application management experts for individual business processes or SAP solutions, such as an application management expert for the personnel administration.

4.3.2 Committee Landscape of SAP CCC

You must also integrate committees into the role model. Similar to the characteristics of the single roles, the design of the committee landscape is also enterprise-specific. However, be sure to always consider already existing structures.

Figure 4.3 uses a customer example to illustrate the structuring of committees regarding SAP decisions across different management levels. This structure enables the centralization of strategic decisions but keeps the local units flexible.

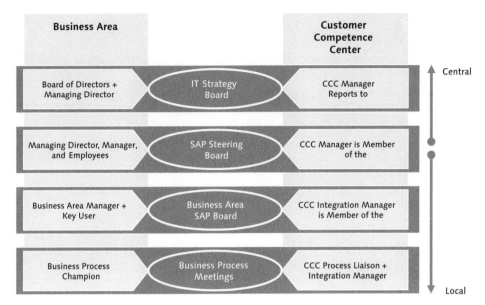

Figure 4.3 Decision Committees – Customer Example

Table 4.1 lists the most important CCC-relevant committees and their typical tasks. The CCC manager must ensure that these committees represent the interests of SAP CCC.

Committee: IT strategy board
▸ Approves strategic specifications, for example, a sourcing strategy
▸ Provides and decides on measures and strategic projects for the orientation of the IT/CCC strategy toward the strategy of the enterprise
▸ Checks risk, revenue, and competitive aspects of IT investments
▸ Creates the necessary basic conditions to achieve the strategic IT/CCC targets
▸ Provides sufficient resources
▸ Checks the progress of strategic IT projects
Committee: SAP steering board
▸ Decides on the amount and usage of expenditures in the SAP environment
▸ Approves plans and budgets for SAP projects, and sets priorities and milestones
▸ Acquires and forwards the appropriate resources
▸ Ensures that enterprise requirements are continuously met and revaluates the business case in projects

Table 4.1 Responsibilities of the CCC-Relevant Committees

▸ Monitors project plans for the delivery of the values and results to be expected in terms of time and budget

▸ Monitors resource and priority conflicts between the business areas and IT functions as well as between the projects

▸ Provides recommendations and submits change requests for strategic plans (priorities, financing, technologies, procedures, resources, etc.)

▸ Communicates strategic goals to the project teams

Committee: IT architecture board

▸ Provides IT architecture guidelines

▸ Monitors relevant new IT developments from the enterprise's point of view

▸ Provides support in complying with the architecture guidelines

▸ Controls the IT architecture design

▸ Ensures that the IT architecture reflects the need for legal and regulatory compliance, the ethical use of information, and the enterprise continuity

▸ Checks compliance with architecture guidelines

Committee: IT process board

▸ Responsible for the process model

▸ Responsible for decisions, enhancement, and maintenance of the process model

▸ Supports process managers

▸ Provides project support and quality assurance

▸ Documents and publishes the process model

▸ Coordinates all process-relevant activities

Table 4.1 Responsibilities of the CCC-Relevant Committees (Cont.)

4.4 Assigning Responsibilities

After you've identified and specified the tasks and roles in the context of SAP CCC, you now need to manage the collaboration of the individual stakeholders in their roles and tasks.

A *responsibility matrix* defines the following issues:

▸ Who makes the decisions

▸ Who is responsible for the execution of tasks

▸ Who is involved to what extent

Figure 4.4 shows a template for a responsibility matrix in the SAP application operation.

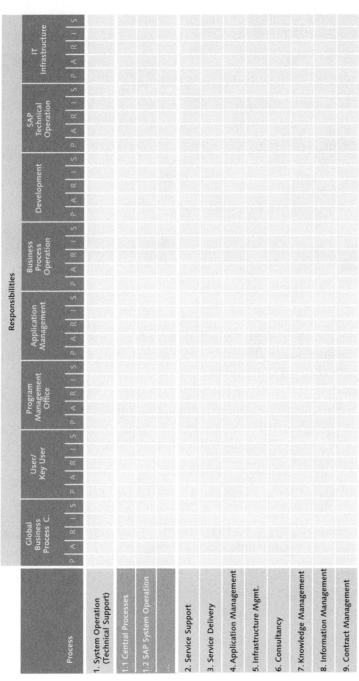

Figure 4.4 Responsibilities Within the SAP Application Operation

Legend: P = Participant; A = Accountable; R = Review; I = Input Required; S = Sign-Off Required

To assign responsibilities, established concepts, such as RACI (**R**esponsible – **A**ccountable – **C**onsulted – **I**nformed) or PARIS (**P**articipant – **A**ccountable – **R**esponsible – **I**nformed – **S**upported), can be used.

The details of the two concepts differ but they include the same basic participatory responsibility types:

▶ **Responsible**
Responsible for a budget, a superordinate project plan or target system, releases (approves).

▶ **Accountable**
Responsible for the execution (those who do the work).

▶ **Consulted**
Involved (those who provide input or whose opinions are sought).

▶ **Informed**
Kept up-to-date (those who are informed about a decision or that a task is completed).

Defining the responsibilities is – particularly in large enterprises – critical for the functioning of the governance approach. In most cases, the range of tasks and freedom of decisions in SAP CCC extend beyond the boundaries of the existing setup or line organization. You must also manage the collaboration between the actors that are positioned in different reporting lines, that is, actors that don't have a multilevel relationship. Because the authorization to do something or decide on something is not defined via the hierarchy, you must specify it in another way, for example, by means of a responsibility matrix.

The SAP scope of tasks is identical in many organizations, but the basic customer-specific conditions are different in terms of the assignment of the tasks to the different organizational units. This concerns particularly the task separation between the business areas and user departments and the IT organization.

The *portfolio analysis* tool provides support in this context. During this process, the individual tasks are categorized by two dimensions, namely, the *application specialization of the tasks* and the required *business process knowledge* (see Figure 4.5).

You can find the tasks that are usually supposed to be assigned to the user department in the upper-right area of the figure. Tasks of the IT organizations are shown in the lower-left area. The dashed lines illustrate the area where the tasks can be assigned in both directions (IT and user department) depending on the enterprise-specific characteristics.

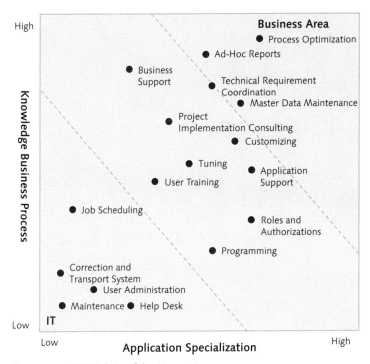

Figure 4.5 SAP Task Portfolio (Excerpt)

4.5 Alternative Organizational Structures

As well as identifying and assigning tasks and roles, you must also develop the structural organization of SAP CCC.

In real-world scenarios, four alternative organizational structures have emerged for SAP CCC (see Figure 4.6):

▶ In *a central SAP CCC*, all tasks and roles are bundled in one organizational unit.

▶ In *multiple decentralized SAP CCCs*, tasks and roles are stored several times. In this context, the most frequently used structuring criterion is the responsibility for a division. However, in many enterprises, the critical mass isn't provided so this organizational structure can't work efficiently.

▶ In a *virtual structure*, SAP CCC is neither located in a central organizational unit nor in several decentralized units. Instead, the tasks and roles are distributed across various organizational units, departments, and employees. This organizational structure requires efficient management and controlling of SAP CCC.

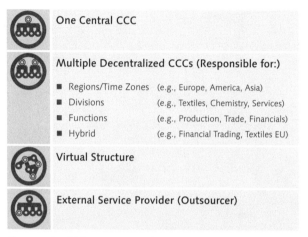

One Central CCC

Multiple Decentralized CCCs (Responsible for:)

- Regions/Time Zones (e.g., Europe, America, Asia)
- Divisions (e.g., Textiles, Chemistry, Services)
- Functions (e.g., Production, Trade, Financials)
- Hybrid (e.g., Financial Trading, Textiles EU)

Virtual Structure

External Service Provider (Outsourcer)

Figure 4.6 CCC Organizational Structures

▶ In the *outsourcing variant*, an external service provider is responsible for the necessary tasks and processes for the customer. This organizational structure isn't used very often because there is no direct access to the potential for innovation and process optimization.

There is no such thing as a generally "valid" organizational structure because the individual conditions vary. However, there is a trend toward the central organization, which can be interpreted as a result of the increasing cost pressure in many industries and as an answer to many organizational acquisition and merger processes.

This is also reflected in a survey among 200 CCC managers that SAP conducted in collaboration with the DSAG (German-Speaking SAP Users' Group). This survey showed that 61% of the participants used a central SAP CCC, 12% used multiple decentralized SAP CCCs, 25% used a virtual structure, and only 1% used an external service provider.

However, both the central and decentralized variants are extreme forms of the organization. To benefit from the respective advantages, most enterprises — particularly large enterprises — use a combination of central and decentralized elements. Figure 4.7 illustrates the characteristics of this federated CCC organization.

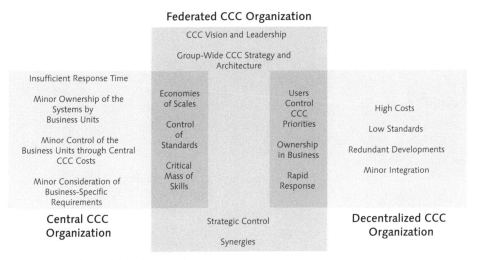

Figure 4.7 Federated CCC Organization

A frequent structuring characteristic of a federated organizational variant is the *geographical dimension*. The real-world example, which is illustrated in Figure 4.8, distinguishes among central, regional, and local responsibilities. This enables customers to define specifications that allow for a high level of standardization even with a small central staff. It also considers the requirement to be able to react to local changes as quickly as possible.

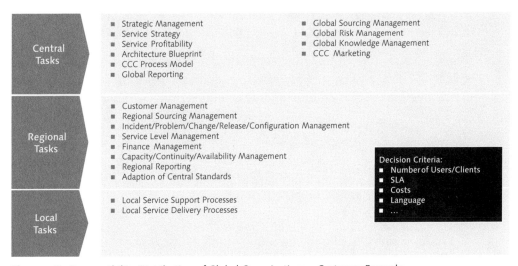

Figure 4.8 Responsibility Distribution of Global Organizations – Customer Example

Table 4.2 compares the respective advantages of the central and decentralized organizational structures.

Advantages of the Central Organizational Structure	Advantages of the Decentralized Organizational Structure
▶ Cost efficient due to the use of economies of scale ▶ Better use of critical resources ▶ Transparent setup and enhancement of IT and process knowledge ▶ Improved efficiency of the support processes ▶ Quality improvement due to standardized and optimized processes ▶ Faster adaptation of the system landscape and increase of the automation level	▶ Quick response to support requests ▶ Fast adaptation to country-specific requirements (e.g., legal requirements, taxes, language) ▶ Competitive approach (internal benchmark) due to decentralized responsibilities ▶ Independent of restrictions of central IT organizations ▶ No language or cultural barriers

Table 4.2 Comparison of Central and Decentralized Organizational Structure of SAP CCC

4.6 Make-or-Buy Decisions

The question often arises concerning which SAP CCC tasks can be assigned to an external service provider as service level-based contracts. Here, we make a distinction between outsourcing and outtasking.

Whereas *outsourcing* refers to the complete transfer of the responsibility for the results of a task area, *outtasking* relates to the transfer of single subtasks within a task area; that is, the end-to-end responsibility remains with the ordering party.

The following objectives are pursued when you decide to receive services from the market:

▶ Reduction of the process complexity

▶ Release of management capacities

▶ Focus on core competencies

▶ Variabilization of cost elements

Figure 4.9 shows an overview of SAP experiences with sourcing strategies in the context of SAP CCC.

The *customer development, technical operation for SAP solutions*, and *IT infrastructure* areas are well suited for an outsourcing model. Proven standards and specifications for the corresponding services require relatively little business process knowledge.

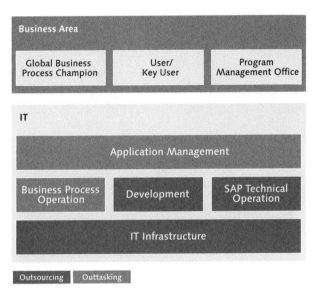

Figure 4.9 Outsourcing Potential in the Application Operation

The *application management* and *operation of business process solutions* areas, however, are usually considered core competencies of SAP CCC. You can assign individual subtasks to an external service provider (outtasking), but SAP CCC remains responsible. Reasons for outtasking in these cases include the following:

▶ Short-term personnel bottlenecks (e.g., for large implementation plans)

▶ Short-term lack of specific competences (e.g., for new SAP technologies)

4.7   Risk Management

The significance of legal and regulatory specifications and conditions has continuously increased in the last years. To ensure *compliance* with external specifications, such as the *Control and Transparency in Business Act* or *Sarbanes-Oxley Act, but also internal standards of the corporate audit, risk management is a central task that has to be defined in the context of the governance of SAP CCC.*

Figure 4.10 illustrates the structure for IT issues in an enterprise using the example of the IT organization.

Figure 4.10 Risk Organization

Note the separation between *risk controlling* and *risk management*. Often, SAP CCC assumes the role of the IT risk manager for application issues. Table 4.3 lists the tasks and responsibilities of IT risk controllers and IT risk managers.

IT Risk Controller
▶ Develops standards with respect to the risk management system
▶ Continuously coordinates risk management
▶ Supports the risk managers to develop and implement measures
▶ Initiates and coordinates cross-IT evaluations of risks and measures
▶ Valuates and presents the risk situation for IT management, group-wide risk management, and external reporting
▶ Continuously coordinates the IT risk management system with the group-wide risk management system

Table 4.3 Responsibilities of the Risk Roles

IT Risk Manager

- Documents the existing risk management system in the form of a risk management guideline that contains a detailed description of the tasks of the persons involved in the risk management process; a documentation of the existing and planned risk management measures, including the responsibilities and dates for the implementations; as well as a documentation of the current risk situation with and without considering existing and planned risk management measures
- Documents the reasons that led to the risk assessments
- Performs risk responsibility and permanent risk control
- Maps the measures, which have been agreed upon with the risk controller, to the measure carriers; communicates the measure carriers and personnel changes regarding the measure carriers to the risk controller
- Defines exact, detailed measures when specification is needed in coordination with the measure carriers, defines implementation dates in coordination with the measure carriers, verifies the measure implementation and adherence to the measure deadlines, communicates measures that haven't been carried out, and communicates deviations from schedules to the risk controller
- Verifies the measure efficiency in coordination with the measure carrier, and communicates inefficient measures to the IT risk controller
- Documents the results of the activities mentioned previously and sends the results to the IT risk controller
- Reports annually in the context of a risk workshop, provides quarterly valuations, and provides ad-hoc reporting
- Implements the risk management standards
- Assesses the risk situation in the specific risk functional area
- Develops proposals for risk KPIs to define threshold values or early indicators for risks and proposals for the quantifiability of the efficiency of measures (in coordination with measure carriers)
- Proposes the control of risks of the risk functional areas and implements measures for risk control
- Acts as contact person for the IT risk controller

Measure Carrier in the Functional Areas

- Specifies the measures in coordination with the risk managers of the risk functional areas
- Assures the measure implementation in the context of the line activities
- Provides regular assessment of the measure efficiency, and develops proposals to improve the measure efficiency

Table 4.3 Responsibilities of the Risk Roles (Cont.)

Measure Carrier in the Functional Areas

▸ Provides appropriate documentation of the measures to ensure the independence of persons of the measures taken (the documentation must particularly ensure that the risk managers can assess the adherence to the measures as well as measure deadlines and measure efficiency)

▸ Develops proposals for risk KPIs to define threshold values or early warning indicators for risks and proposals for the quantifiability of the efficiency of measures (in coordination with IT risk managers)

Table 4.3 Responsibilities of the Risk Roles (Cont.)

There are numerous risk management standards that must be known and managed in SAP CCC. The following list describes some examples of the main standards.

▸ The *Sarbanes-Oxley Act* (SOX) is a law enacted in the United States to support the confidence of the investors by subjecting publicly traded enterprises to a strengthened auditing system.

▸ The *COSO Framework* has been developed by the Committee of Sponsoring Organizations of the Treadway Commission (COSO) to carry out internal controls. It also serves as a tool to monitor the internal control system.

▸ *CobiT* (Control Objectives for Information and Related Technology) provides a framework for the process-oriented control of IT's trustworthiness and quality. Moreover, it is supposed to function as a link between the COSO and ITIL frameworks.

▸ *ISO Standard 17799* ensures an appropriate security of the information in an enterprise by providing best practices for guidelines, methods, processes, roles, and responsibilities.

4.8   Standard Documents

Governance is a tool to implement the strategy of SAP CCC. To get the plans and standards operational, specific standard documents have proved their worth in CCC real-world scenarios.

In addition to numerous documents that SAP directly provides (e.g., installation instructions), you must usually also manage customer-specific and solution-specific characteristics. Table 4.4 contains an overview of a set of documents that has proven advantageous in the operation of SAP CCC.

Document Name	Main Content
Business process model	▶ Customer process model ▶ SAP reference model ▶ Implementation model ▶ Modeling methodology ▶ Modeling tools
Organizational change management concept (OCM concept)	▶ Current situation ▶ OCM goals ▶ OCM target groups ▶ Messages ▶ OCM strategy ▶ OCM KPIs ▶ Prerequisites ▶ OCM budget ▶ OCM controlling
IT security concept	▶ Guidelines ▶ Data protection ▶ Audits
Master data concept	▶ Definition of the master data structures and their integration ▶ Master data maintenance processes
Software logistics concept	▶ System architecture ▶ Client concept ▶ Transport strategy ▶ System and client parameterization
Migration concept	▶ Actual and planned development plan ▶ Migration environment ▶ Migration procedure ▶ Implementation standards ▶ Migration tools

Table 4.4 Critical Documents for the Operation of SAP CCC

Document Name	Main Content
Role and authorization concept	▶ Organizational structure ▶ Process structure ▶ Security requirements ▶ Roles ▶ User types ▶ Naming conventions
Training concept	▶ Methodical didactic framework ▶ Training overview ▶ Training planning ▶ Training content ▶ Training documents
Test concept	▶ Test design ▶ Test environments (processes, organization, tools) ▶ Test data strategy ▶ Templates for test cases
Programming guideline	▶ Guidelines for: ▶ Customizing ▶ Customer development ▶ Enhancements ▶ Modifications
Archiving concept	▶ Archiving objects ▶ Archiving process ▶ Archiving planning
CCC service manual	▶ IT service model ▶ IT service glossary ▶ IT service standard processes ▶ Architecture
CCC service concept	▶ Specification of the CCC service manual for specific IT services/IT systems ▶ Service level

Table 4.4 Critical Documents for the Operation of SAP CCC (Cont.)

You should provide a *document profile* (see Figure 4.11) for each document that defines issues of focus areas in the content and responsibilities prior to the creation of the actual document. It is also necessary to define binding naming conventions for documents, storage structure, and locations. SAP Solution Manager (particularly for implementation documents) and SAP NetWeaver Portal Knowledge Management (e.g., for CCC service manuals) are useful for the storage of documents in this context.

Document Name:	Master data concept
Document Created by:	J. Doe
Responsible for Document:	J. Doe
Content of the Document:	...
Scope of the Document:	This document is binding for all employees in the enterprise.
Documentation Structure:	...
Document Category:	The document is an Excel table (.xls).
Storage Location:	The document is stored in SAP Solution Manager and centrally accessible for all.

Figure 4.11 Document Profile

As shown in Figure 4.12, the provision or update of the concepts mentioned follows the phases of the SAP procedure model for the implementation of SAP application systems. The presentation takes into account that you must provide the respective concepts at defined points in time. For example, an updated master data concept must be made available before you enter the *implementation* phase.

For project and user documentation, SAP suggests the RWD Info Pak Suite. RWD Info Pak is a cost-effective solution that automatically records the individual steps of the processes in the SAP application during operations. As a result, you are provided with a Microsoft Word document that is formatted according to your own requirements. You can then add specific notes for the users on the usual Word interface.

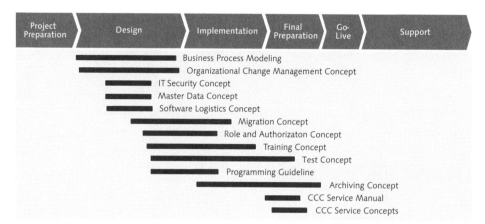

Figure 4.12 Creation Times of Critical Documents

4.9 Summary

A governance model for SAP CCC serves to implement the strategic objectives because it defines the framework and the main functions of SAP CCC as well as the involved roles. Furthermore, responsibilities manage the mapping of roles to functions; that is, they provide information on the tasks of the individual persons.

The governance for SAP CCC is also responsible for specifying the basic organizational structure. Depending on the enterprise, the structure may vary from a completely central SAP CCC, to decentralized and virtual organizational structures, to a complete outsourcing to an external service provider.

Finally, the governance model — in the context of risk management — must also ensure that the enterprise considers all legal and regulatory specifications (compliance).

Usually, numerous standard documents that are supposed to be used in daily operations specify the framework of a governance model for SAP CCC.

5   Processes of SAP CCC

Based on the SAP CCC strategy and the governance model for implementing this strategy, the process organization's goal is to define and describe the most critical processes.

For this purpose, the CCC process model includes the most essential reference processes according to the IT Infrastructure Library (ITIL).

SAP provides the *SAP Standards for Solution Operations* for the SAP application operation. These guidelines enable the CCC organization to proactively support the essential business processes. You can find an overview of the initial standards and their structuring in Section 5.2.

Then, selected processes are described that can typically be found in real-world scenarios. These include the *service level management* (SLM) as a critical factor for establishing an organization with a customer and service orientation.

Because the CCC certification (see Section 9.3) is a fundamental milestone for setting up SAP CCC, we describe the four areas relevant for certification:

► Service Desk
► Information management
► Contract management
► Coordination of development requests

The chapter concludes with procedure for developing individual process models in your enterprise.

5.1   Process Model

After the tasks of SAP CCC have been identified by means of governance, the process organization transfers the tasks to individual processes and controls their relationships to one another. The *process model* can be used by the various stakeholders as a reference to processes and activities to create a common understanding.

Figure 5.1 shows the SAP recommendation for an SAP CCC process model. This process model is based on practical experience and considers the terms and structures of the new ITIL version 3.

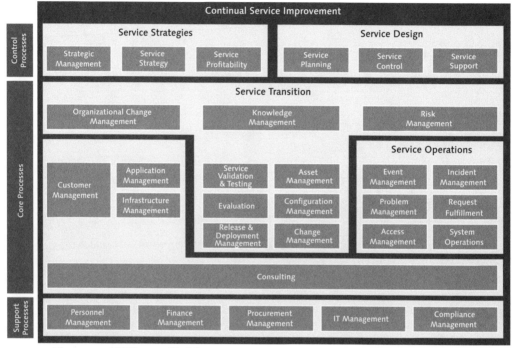

Figure 5.1 CCC Process Model

The process model is subdivided into *process groups*, that is, control processes, core processes, and support processes.

▶ *Control processes* are activities that define, monitor, and control the core and support processes. Essential processes of this group are the *service strategy* and *service design*.

▶ *Core processes* comprise the value-added activities of SAP CCC. Processes of this group are oriented toward the benefit for the enterprise. It particularly includes *service transition* and *service operations*.

▶ *Support processes* are used to ensure that core processes are run as smoothly and efficiently as possible.

The individual processes are introduced briefly in the next sections. Note that the process model only serves as a reference and must be adapted individually to the enterprise's conditions.

5.1.1 Control Processes of SAP CCC

Table 5.1 illustrates the processes required for controlling the CCC activities.

Processes	Activities	Results	Success Factors
Strategic management	▶ Development and continuous improvement of the CCC strategy ▶ Coordination with the involved business areas	▶ Currently communicated CCC vision and CCC strategy ▶ Current strategy document	▶ Participation of the top management ▶ Far-reaching integration with the enterprise
Service strategy	▶ Definition of CCC customers ▶ Development of CCC offers	▶ Development and updating of the service strategy	▶ Established customer relationship management
Service profitability	▶ IT cost management and activity allocation ▶ Implementation of preinvestment analyses ▶ Service portfolio management ▶ Requirements management	▶ CCC service portfolio ▶ Cost and benefit transparency of the CCC services ▶ Targeted activity allocation	▶ Prove for the value contribution of the CCC services ▶ Establishing a TCO model, determining and updating TCO
Service planning	▶ Determination of a service catalog ▶ Definition of the service engineering process	▶ CCC service catalog	▶ Service engineering process defined by the various business areas

Table 5.1 Control Processes in SAP CCC

Processes	Activities	Results	Success Factors
Service control	▶ Definition of committees ▶ Definition of the measure system ▶ Provision of information to support the decision-making processes	▶ Established committees ▶ Key figure-supported control of all CCC activities	▶ Value-oriented control
Service support	▶ Service catalog management ▶ Capacity management ▶ Availability management ▶ Service continuity management ▶ Information security management ▶ Supplier management	▶ Long-term planning and optimization of the CCC services	▶ Synchronization of the service delivery processes in a service planning

Table 5.1 Control Processes in SAP CCC (Cont.)

5.1.2 Core Processes of SAP CCC

The core processes described in Table 5.2 must be taken into consideration for establishing SAP CCC.

Processes	Activities	Results	Success factors
Customer management	▶ Customer contact management ▶ Key account management ▶ Customer relationship management ▶ Complaint handling	▶ Customer-focused service provision	▶ Customer and service orientation of CCC employees

Table 5.2 Core Processes of SAP CCC

Processes	Activities	Results	Success factors
Application management	▸ Provisioning of applications ▸ Requirement ▸ Design ▸ Implementation ▸ Delivery ▸ Operations ▸ Optimization	▸ Application according to customer requirement ▸ Optimal IT support of business processes	▸ Synchronization with IT service management processes
Infrastructure management	▸ Provision of IT infrastructure solutions ▸ Design and planning ▸ Setup ▸ Operations ▸ Support	▸ Service level-based IT infrastructure	▸ Defined standards
Service validation and testing	▸ Validation and testing of existing services ▸ Implementation of tests	▸ Quality-assured CCC services	▸ Synchronization of test activities ▸ High level of test automation
Evaluation	▸ Assessment of the service quality ▸ Implementation of measures to ensure and improve the service quality	▸ Evaluated CCC services	▸ Evaluation by external auditors
Release and deployment management	▸ Extensive hardware and software implementations ▸ Planning functional packages by reconciling department requirements with what is technically possible	▸ Release plan/calendar ▸ Checklist for launching releases	▸ Adjustment of the release frequency to program phases

Table 5.2 Core Processes of SAP CCC (Cont.)

Processes	Activities	Results	Success factors
Asset management	▶ Planning, control, and maintenance of asset data (e.g., licenses, contracts, depreciation, cost centers, budgets)	▶ Transparency of the IT assets costs	▶ Integration with the configuration management
Configuration management	▶ Planning and control of configuration data ▶ Selection and identification of all configuration elements ▶ Determination and authorization of accepted configuration elements	▶ Central information basis	▶ Comprehensive understanding of all functions
Change management	▶ Provision of standardized methods for efficient handling of all changes ▶ Initiation, documentation, and authorization of changes ▶ Estimation of the effects, costs, benefits, and risks of changes ▶ Change releases ▶ Planning, coordination, and implementation of changes ▶ Review of changes	▶ Effective, efficient, and safe implementation of changes	▶ Communication of change planning to business areas
Event management	▶ Definition and setup of threshold values ▶ Continuous monitoring ▶ Forwarding of threshold value deviations	▶ Notification of threshold value deviations	▶ Integration with incident management ▶ High level of automation for necessary activities

Table 5.2 Core Processes of SAP CCC (Cont.)

Processes	Activities	Results	Success factors
Incident management	► Tracking of incidents and entry of incident reports ► Classification of all incidents and immediate support ► Determination and diagnosis ► Troubleshooting and recovery ► Completing the incident ► Responsibility for the incident and monitoring, tracking, and communicating in conjunction with the incident	► Quickest possible recovery of the normal service operation	► Key user concept ► Integration with the problem management and change management
Problem management	► Troubleshooting ► Problem solving ► Support for handling serious incidents ► Proactive problem prevention	► Reduction of error effects ► Proactive prevention of incidents, problems, and errors	► Integration with incident management
Request fulfillment	► Collection of business requirements ► Development of services according to the business requirements ► Monitoring of requirement fulfillment	► "Pipeline" with service projects ► Structured and evaluated requirements	► Proactivity toward business areas ► Clear communication of existing services
Access management	► Control of the authorization distribution ► Maintenance of authorizations	► Authorization concept	► Clear communication of the authorization concept to all business areas

Table 5.2 Core Processes of SAP CCC (Cont.)

Processes	Activities	Results	Success factors
System operations	▶ Securing the standard tasks of the system operation (e.g., IT monitoring, job scheduling, etc.)	▶ Effective and efficient operation of the SAP solutions	▶ High level of automation through effective tool support
Organizational change management	▶ Implementation of IT-related organizational changes ▶ Support of the specialist areas for the implementation of organizational changes	▶ Marketing plan ▶ Communication plan	▶ Clear, simple messages ▶ Communication of the added value of the organizational change
Knowledge management	▶ Implementation of measures for intercompany knowledge transfer ▶ Reconciliation of the knowledge to be transferred with the specialist areas	▶ Plan for successful knowledge exchange	▶ Companywide system for knowledge management
Risk management	▶ Minimization of risks for implementing control mechanisms	▶ Control mechanisms ▶ Minimization of risks	▶ Reconciliation with all business areas
Consulting	▶ Consultation for topics, such as business processes, SAP solutions, project methodologies	▶ Knowledge transfer for SAP solutions	▶ Active customer and information management

Table 5.2 Core Processes of SAP CCC (Cont.)

5.1.3 Support Processes

Support processes (e.g., the procurement management) are controlled independent of CCC in most organizations. For this reason, their description is omitted here.

5.2   Process Standards for SAP Application Operation

SAP Standards for Solution Operations are guidelines used for the efficient operation of critical business applications. With these standards, SAP documents its compiled experience for planning, providing, supporting, and increasing the efficiency of IT services within the SAP environment. At the same time, SAP ensures that these standards are supported by suitable tools, in particular by SAP Solution Manager.

The standards are available for all customers in the SAP Service Marketplace under *service.sap.com/supportstandards*.

The standards refer to the roles of the SAP application operation model illustrated in Figure 4.1 in Chapter 4.

Among others, the following standards are defined:

▶ **Change request management**
Enables an efficient and on-time implementation of changes throughout the system landscape with minimal risks.

▶ **Change control management**
Allows for the central monitoring and comparison of different statuses with regard to changes in the various technical components, parameters, and so on that concern a business process.

▶ **Exception handling**
Describes a model and central system landscape-wide procedures for managing exceptions and error situations.

▶ **Business process and interface monitoring**
Describes the integrated monitoring and control of business-critical business processes.

▶ **Data integrity**
Prevents data inconsistencies between the various elements of a solution.

▶ **Transactional consistency**
Ensures the data synchronization of applications from distributed system landscapes.

▶ **Data volume management**
Defines the management of data growth.

► **Enterprise SOA readiness**
Covers both the organizational and technical readiness for the use of an enterprise service-oriented architecture (enterprise SOA).

► **Incident management**
Describes the process for the solution of incidents.

► **Job scheduling management**
Explains the management of planning, scheduling, and monitoring of background jobs in the system landscape.

► **Remote supportability**
Describes the basic prerequisites for optimizing the maintenance of customer solutions.

► **Root cause analysis**
Defines the procedure of an end-to-end root cause analysis across different support levels and different technologies.

► **System administration**
Specifies the administration of SAP technologies to efficiently operate customer solutions.

► **System monitoring**
Details the monitoring and reporting of IT solutions.

► **Upgrade**
Defines best practices in release management.

► **Minimum documentation**
Defines the required documentation and evaluation with regard to customer solutions.

These as well as other SAP-defined standards follow a transparent repetitive structure: After the standard and its interfaces have been mapped for the SAP solution operation, the process and tasks of the individual roles are described. Recommendations for supporting the procedure by means of suitable tools enable you to implement the process efficiently and in a timely manner. The standards are rounded off by recommendations for the implementation procedure.

5.3   Service Level Management

In many enterprises, SAP solutions form an integral part of business-critical processes. Therefore, the process for migrating individual customer requirements must be professionally implemented in standardized, competitive, and flexible CCC services. In this context, the focus must be on business, organizational, technical, and legal requirements. The design of CCC services decisively influences the industrialization of the CCC processes and consequently the efficiency and effectiveness of the CCC organization.

5.3.1   Targets of the Service Level Management

Service level management (SLM) bundles subprocesses that ensure the development, stipulation, documentation, and monitoring of service and operational level agreements (SLA and OLA) as well as underpinning contracts (UC). The establishment of an SLM is a key success factor for customer satisfaction, professional control of the CCC organization, and reduction of the total cost of ownership (TCO).

The implementation of this process has the following targets:

- ▶ Implementing the customer expectation
- ▶ Controlling the CCC resources
- ▶ Improving internal marketing
- ▶ Supporting active cost control

5.3.2   Implementing the Customer Expectations

SLM requires and supports the dialogue between customers and the CCC organization as well as the transparency of possibly varying interests. The business area can show how CCC services can ensure the business targets. At the same time, the CCC organization can illustrate how CCC services emerge and which costs are associated with the different service qualities. By reconciling the interests and stipulating SLAs, you can avoid unrealistic expectations.

5.3.3   Controlling the CCC Resources

Determining and actively monitoring SLAs enables you to lay the foundations for medium- and long-term capacity planning and resource control. Consequently, you can recognize bottlenecks in time and develop solution scenarios in cooperation with the business areas. In many customer organizations, this not only affects the infrastructure resources but also particularly the staff competencies.

5.3.4 Internal Marketing

Within the framework of monthly reviews or through continuous service level reporting, the performance of the CCC organization is mapped transparently, and SAP CCC is implemented by the business areas according to the motto: "Do good and talk about it."

5.3.5 Cost Control

The requirements of services are complex — they must be plannable, adjustable, contractually controllable, calculable, and finally billable. If the cost accounting and service allocation have a high degree of maturity and if the service costs can be mapped transparently for the business areas, you can increase the cost awareness, which, in turn, influences the behavior of the customers and users.

5.3.6 Responsibilities and Obligations

SLM describes the process of how you define, negotiate, implement, and control IT services. The starting point is always the determination and stipulation of the business areas' requirement. These are then transferred to the services with the corresponding qualities and documented and published in a service catalog. You must note here that agreed-upon service qualities can be monitored and reported automatically. Don't negotiate service levels that you can't measure.

The service level and the cost allocation are continuously determined and reported based on the agreements. In the reporting, SAP CCC checks the quality of third-party vendors that are required for providing the services. Improving service quality should be considered a continuous task of SLM. Achieved cost benefits, for example, through decreasing storage costs, must be forwarded to the business areas promptly.

5.3.7 Establishment Procedure

The following descriptions show the possible steps for setting up SLM within your organization.

SLM implementations require an interdisciplinary team from the business areas and SAP CCC. They should define the role of the future service level manager already at the beginning because he could assume the responsibility for the implementation process.

Customers hardly ever start an implementation from scratch. Consequently, an assessment of customer satisfaction, current services, processes, and reporting tools can help you consider past experience and determine a starting point for planning.

The precise structuring and definition of services is fundamental for designing the SLAs later. They arrange the objective measurement data for the performance as well as the competences and responsibilities of the contract parties. Figure 5.2 shows a simple SAP application services structure that offers multiple variants of service categories based on the different requirements. The provision of different service categories only makes sense, however, if they use different processes and resources to ensure usage-dependent cost and activity allocation.

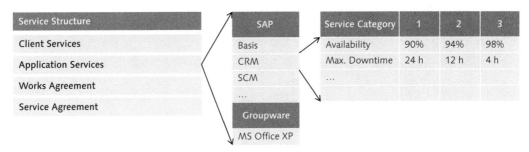

Figure 5.2 Service Structure

You must concentrate on customer- and service-oriented service levels. Users won't understand it if you report the availability of infrastructure components while the application doesn't work. Possible service levels for the application operation should therefore not refer to key figures that relate to business processes:

▶ Availability and performance of the application

▶ Downtime per incident

▶ Response time for troubleshooting

Table 5.3 includes the general structure for defining a service level based on the example for the availability of the *Internet sales* business process. After you've defined the CCC services and their measurement criteria and successfully stipulated them between the business area and SAP CCC, you must map them in the organization, processes, and tools.

Description Parameter	Example: Availability Internet Sales
Measurement parameter	Determines whether the Internet sales application is available for the users
Reference value	Technical components of the Internet sales business process — determined using the *component failure impact analysis* method (CFIA)
Measurement criterion	Selected transactions, for example, orders, implemented with defined response behavior
Measurement period	24/7
Measurement interval	Every 5 minutes
Measurement procedure	Relevant data collected in SAP Customer Relationship Management (SAP CRM) and centrally processed by SAP Solution Manager
Measurement points	Central monitoring in SAP Solution Manager
Measurement value	Percentage value
Transfer of data	Via service level reporting
Evaluation interval	Monthly evaluations

Table 5.3 SLA Report – Example Availability of SAP CRM

The SAP Solution Manager tool comprehensively maps the relevant service level of the SAP solution operation [Anderhub 06].

5.4 Service Desk and Incident Management

Incidents that occur during the operation of business-critical applications can result in considerable losses, if it's not possible to treat the incidents correctly, identify their causes, and minimize their effect through immediate measures. *Service desk management* as well as *incident management* define the process and the tools to control the collaboration of the participating support instances and to resolve incidents promptly.

5.4.1 Targets of Service Desk and Incident Management

The primary target of the support organization is to create effective and efficient support processes for the users of SAP solutions to recover the normal service operation as fast as possible after an incident has occurred. This requires the seamless integration of all support units and the support of procedures through high-performance tools. The processes must be designed to ensure a fast assignment of suitable specialists to the respective problems.

The implementation of this process has the following targets:

▶ Simple generation of incident reports

▶ Use of effective tools for fast problem solutions

▶ Smooth cooperation with SAP Active Global Support (SAP AGS)

▶ Identification of improvement potentials

5.4.2 Simple Incident Report

The first step for processing incidents effectively and in a targeted manner is to create incident reports including all relevant context information in an uncomplicated manner. You should provide different report options. Each report should provide technical data, such as system ID, client, support package version, and the transaction in the background, in addition to the initial prioritization and problem description. This minimizes the number of queries from downstream support units to the reporting person and accelerates the support process.

5.4.3 Use of Effective Tools

Based on the information about the SAP components, the priority, and the category, the reports should be automatically assigned to a defined support unit. For processing incidents, you must set up your own solution databases and enable the use of the manufacturers' databases. In addition, diagnostic tools reduce the troubleshooting time, which increases the availability of the IT solutions and minimizes negative business influences.

5.4.4   Smooth Cooperation with SAP

You can forward SAP problems that can't be solved with customer-specific support units to SAP AGS. The more detailed the information about the incident is and the faster SAP can access the customer environment, for example, via remote service connections, the faster SAP can provide a solution.

5.4.5   Identification of Improvement Potentials

A professional incident management lays the foundation to identify improvement potentials. They refer to supported business processes and IT service and application management processes, the improvement of customer satisfaction, the identification of training needs for users and support employees, as well as the determination of gaps in the business process or system documentation.

5.4.6   Responsibilities and Obligations

An optimized incident management process results in high customer satisfaction. The following sections provide a detailed description of this process because it identifies optimization potentials in many customer organizations. The described process requires the use of SAP Solution Manager Service Desk.

Creating Messages

There are different ways to create a message:

▶ Users can create an incident report directly from the transaction in which the error occurred.

▶ Users can contact the assigned key user. If the key user can't answer the question, he creates a support message in SAP Solution Manager.

▶ Another option is to create the message via an Internet-based user interface (IC WebClient) and a URL in the browser outside SAP Solution Manager.

Attachments, for example, screenshots of an entry screen, can't be inserted in the support message. By saving the support message, it's automatically sent to the Service Desk of SAP Solution Manager.

Distributing Messages

The support message can then be called in Service Desk. There, the message is automatically assigned to the previously defined best possible support unit.

Processing Messages

Employees that are responsible for further processing can be notified via email, fax, or text messages. The assignment of messages is implemented by a background processing and simultaneous condition control, which enables the start of an SAP workflow. The interaction of workflow and approval enables you to selectively lock or send messages to SAP.

Inbound messages and the status of the messages can be monitored in the Service Desk anytime.

After you select a message to be processed, you have different tools and functions to choose from for processing:

▶ **Solution database**
The customer-specific solution database is the first source where you can search for already existing solutions for the described problem. This solution database is empty initially and is filled successively by the support organization. In the course of time, the database is filled with problems and corresponding solutions and thus becomes a useful and time-saving tool because the customer's support organization can use it to search for SAP Notes and Service Desk documents, for example. The solution database uses a classification method that you can use to search according to subjects, solution types, symptoms, and attributes, such as release information. The Service Desk implementation enables you to extend the standard functions with customer-specific search criteria.

▶ **SAP Notes search in the SAP Service Marketplace**
If the problem has never occurred in the enterprise before and can't be found in the solution database, the Service Desk employee can search for SAP Notes directly from the message. The implementation of the SAP Notes search by means of Service Desk is considerably more effective than a manual search in

the SAP Service Marketplace because the search criteria are automatically filled as soon as the data of the message is used.

▶ **Diagnosis**
The cause for incidents can be localized and diagnosed by means of SAP Solution Manager's root cause analysis. Here, applications that are not based on ABAP technologies, such as Java or .NET, are supported as well.

▶ **Forwarding messages**
If you can't find a suitable SAP Note in the SAP Service Marketplace, you create an internal note in the message describing the previous solution attempts and forward the problem message to the downstream support unit. The forwarding is done manually in the Service Desk. Each Service Desk employee can forward messages to another support unit. If required, you can restrict the recipient group to which the messages can be sent.

Forwarding messages to SAP is controlled via an authorization object. The appropriate configuration enables you to automatically forward messages to SAP.

▶ **Forwarding messages to external Service Desks**
As of Release 4.0, SAP Solution Manager includes an open interface for exchanging messages with help desk systems of other manufacturers. This enables the bidirectional exchange of messages with the relevant information, such as priority, SAP category, and SAP components via Web Services to ensure a simple, flexible, and platform-independent operation.

▶ **Cooperation with SAP AGS**
One of the unique features of Service Desk in SAP Solution Manager is the option to cooperate with SAP AGS to achieve shorter solution times. SAP AGS receives targeted information for improved message processing. If the different support units of the customer's support organization can't solve the problem, you can send the support message to SAP AGS. Remote service connections are essential components in this cooperation because they enable SAP AGS to access your system to comprehend the problem within its specific environment.

Delivering the Solution

Depending on the structure of your support processes, either SAP AGS or the support organization of your service provider processes the messages and returns them together with the recommended solution or a question and the current status. If a solution is proposed, it becomes visible in the transaction monitor, and the support employees receive an email notification, provided that this option has been activated. The support employee evaluates the solution and triggers a *change request*, if required. When the solution has been implemented, the support employee notifies the creator of the message about the changed message status. At this point, the message creator checks the solution and confirms it.

Confirming the Message

The Service Desk employee closes the message and documents the solution for the internal solution database so that other support employees can access this solution.

5.4.7 Procedure for Establishing an End-to-End Support Process

The implementation of an end-to-end support process requires the cooperation of process, technology, and organization. SAP Solution Manager Service Desk provides a preconfigured solution for this purpose that is based on the ITIL process standard and is optimized for SAP-specific support request. The customer organization can implement the problem solution process optionally in three to four support levels. SAP recommends the use of three support levels for SAP customers *without* SAP CCC and four support levels for customers *with* SAP CCC. The architecture is structured as follows:

1. **First-level support**
   The first-level support is the central contact person for users. The first-level support consists of key users or designated satellite system users that work with SAP Solution Manager.

2. **Second-level support**
   The second-level support comprises application and technology experts that are familiar with the details of the customer-specific applications and business processes.

3. **Third-level support (CCC level)**
   Typical activities of the third-level support are the search for SAP Notes and the use of the solution database. Responsibilities of the third-level support generally depend on the size of the enterprise. For smaller enterprises and customers without SAP CCC, these tasks are assumed in the second-level support.

4. **Fourth-level support (SAP AGS)**
   SAP AGS is the last level of the problem solution process for all customers if the problem can't be solved by the customers themselves.

This structure enables an efficient control and solution of incident reports.

For measuring the quality of the support processes, the Service Desk of SAP Solution Manager provides various profiles for SLAs. These can be tailored to the specific requirements of the customers.

After the service levels and their roles have been defined, the CCC organization needs to plan the necessary personnel capacities. The calculation is influenced by various factors:

▶ Number of users

▶ Types of user (e.g., self-service user, full-time user)

▶ Service level (particularly service times)

▶ Number of countries

▶ Number of SAP modules/components

▶ Others

Due to the many factors, you can't specify a general formula or recommendation for calculating the necessary CCC personnel capacities. Individual analyses are the best solutions. Figure 5.3 shows a distribution of incident reports to support units based on the available benchmark data.

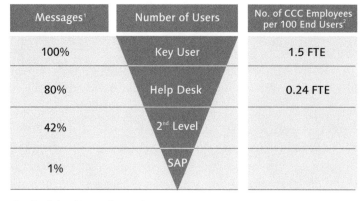

Messages[1]	Number of Users	No. of CCC Employees per 100 End Users[2]
100%	Key User	1.5 FTE
80%	Help Desk	0.24 FTE
42%	2nd Level	
1%	SAP	

[1] Number of Inbound Messages (Percentage)
[2] Example: SAP R/3 – HR; SAP Benchmark 2004

Figure 5.3 Distributing Incident Reports to Support Units

Figure 5.4 illustrates the ratio of SAP users to SAP CCC employees.

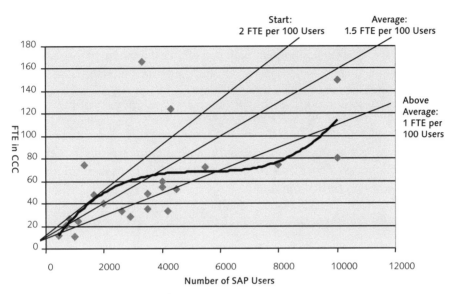

Figure 5.4 Benchmark CCC Employees

The number of required employees (*Full Time Equivalent* = FTEs) per 100 users mainly depends on the degree of maturity of SAP CCC (start, average, above average). The illustrated levels differentiate CCC organizations that are in the setup phase (start) through to organizations with 1.5 to 2.5 years of experience that have put in extensive efforts to optimize processes and to train support employees.

5.5   Information Management

In the following sections, the term *information management* also subsumes the tasks of information and knowledge management and marketing. No distinction is made between internal and external marketing.

5.5.1   Goal of Information Management

Information management is positioned insufficiently in many CCC organizations. However, professionally implemented information management serves several goals:

▶ **Knowledge transfer via SAP solutions**
The targeted and prompt preparation and forwarding of information by means of solutions, best practices, and planning within the SAP environment both to the business areas and within the IT organization is the prerequisite for necessary strategic decisions, sound planning, and effective implementations. In this context, the CCC organization serves as an information filter because it only forwards enterprise-relevant information to the respective target groups.

▶ **Increase in acceptance of SAP solutions**
Information and communication are the most powerful and most effective organizational change management instruments and are essential for the success of new initiatives, such as SAP implementation projects, new solutions, or new procedures. Information about changes must always include the associated benefits. Only then can the required acceptance be achieved and resistance reduced.

▶ **Increase in acceptance of the CCC organization**
The active marketing of SAP competencies and the services of the CCC organization support the internal and external positioning and improve the organization's image. A good positioning ensures that the CCC organization is recognized as a consultant and initial contact for SAP issues by the management and the business areas.

5.5.2 Establishment Procedure

A structured procedure results in an integrated marketing concept with clearly defined target groups, messages, and suitable instruments. This procedure is subdivided into four steps as shown in Figure 5.5.

In the first step, you must define the *marketing strategy*, which is derived from the business and CCC strategy. It should consider the following points:

▶ **Market orientation at four levels**
At the *market field strategy* level, the product/market combinations are determined. In this context, market penetration, market development, product development, and diversification are important. The second level, *market stimulation*, defines how the market is influenced by the preference, for example. This means that a strong differentiation increases the demand for CCC services. The *market fragmentation* level defines the scope. In most customer organizations, this restricts to a defined fractional segment in the form of the specific

enterprise. The *market area* is the fourth level and defines the local orientation. In this context, many CCC organizations show a tendency toward internationalization within the framework of centralization, that is, the global provision of CCC services via a central organization.

▶ **Customer orientation**
Many customer-oriented strategies are possible for positioning the CCC organization. Depending on the strategic orientation of the enterprise, you must differentiate between innovation orientation, quality orientation, trademark orientation, and cost orientation. Against the background of the ever-increasing need for differentiation, innovative approaches become more significant.

▶ **Unique selling point**
Consider how you can distinguish the CCC organization from potential competitors, such as external consulting firms, or which areas of the CCC organization feature competitive advantages. This can be, for instance, detailed knowledge of the business processes.

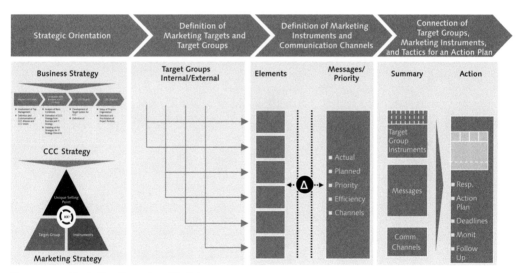

Figure 5.5 Marketing Procedure Model

In a second step, you define the targets and target groups of marketing. The marketing targets are derived from the CCC strategy and the targets of SAP CCC. These guidelines must be specifically implemented and supported by the marketing department. Moreover, you must define clear target groups, both internal and external. In the third step, you select the marketing instruments and the available communication channels.

You should preferably use a *marketing mix* that consists of various marketing instruments. In this context, the classic "7P's" of marketing are used. The "7P's" are factors that can be influenced by SAP CCC for marketing purposes:

▶ Product/service

▶ Price/cost performance ratio

▶ Promotion

▶ Place/customers

▶ People (e.g., skills)

▶ Physical facilities (e.g., tool authority)

▶ Process management

To increase the influence of these marketing instruments and to reduce the costs, you must select the marketing channels cleverly. Figure 5.6 shows an example of the different marketing channels that are available in SAP CCC as well as their costs and benefit or purpose.

Communication Channel	Relevance (Example)	Costs	Purpose
Email, e.g., Newsletter		Low	Content Reaches the Defined Target Group. Fast and Cost-Efficient. Push Information.
Intranet/Internet/Extranet		Low	Presentation of Areas/Services. Pull Information.
Print Product		Medium	Presentation of Project Results for Specific Purposes (e.g., Congress, Trade Shows).
Telco/Web Conferences		Low	Addressing of Small Target Groups for New Information. Often Used for Expert Discussions. Low Costs – World-Wide Availability, if Required.
Management Seminars		Medium	Presentation of CCC in Management Seminars.
Meetings/Workshops		Medium to High	Addressing of Small Target Groups in order to Produce Results.
Enterprise TV		Medium	Reaches all Employees. Short and Clear Messages.
Enterprise Radio		Medium	Doesn't Reach a Defined Target Group. Potential for High Level of Attention.

Figure 5.6 Marketing Channels

The last step is to develop an action plan, which is derived from a summary of steps one to three. You determine the target groups, the marketing instruments to be used, and a schedule. In this context, it's important that you clearly define the responsibilities to ensure the success of the marketing campaign.

You can access an SAP tool via SAP NetWeaver Portal that supports you and your customers in processing, providing, and searching information (*http://www.sap.com/platform/netweaver/components/portal/index.epx*).

5.6 Contract Management

Contract management controls the contractual interaction of the CCC organization with SAP. It provides the customer's central contacts for SAP that have corresponding competences.

5.6.1 Goals of Contract Management

Contract management bundles all contract-relevant activities and ensures that legal regulations and contractual regulations with SAP, other partners, and vendors are observed. This includes product, license, maintenance, and consultancy contracts as well as SLAs.

5.6.2 Responsibilities and Obligations

When setting up contract management, you must consider the following responsibilities and obligations:

▸ **SAP remote service connection**
The remote connection is an essential tool for the interaction between the CCC organization and SAP and for prompt problem solutions. The basic task of contract management is to initially establish the connection and to continuously maintain and manage it.

▸ **Access to SAP information and tools**
To channel the activities, established identity management is mandatory, that is, maintaining and administering authorizations for accessing SAP information tools.

▸ **Maintaining customer data for SAP**
The up-to-date maintenance of necessary and useful data (SAP release, components, production data, contact data, and so on) ensures fast and targeted processing of requests and problems.

▶ **Ordering and distributing software**
To avoid unused SAP licenses, you should centrally coordinate the purchase and distribution of SAP software within the enterprise.

▶ **SAP Services**
This area of responsibility includes planning, purchasing, and administering SAP Services, such as SAP consulting services, SAP training, and SAP support services.

▶ **Access to SAP solutions for third parties**
If third parties require access to SAP solutions, you must also ensure the maintenance and administration for these connections.

▶ **Purchasing and distributing software, hardware, middleware, and services from third parties**
You need to establish processes within the customer organization that manage the coordination of requests, purchases, distribution, and maintenance of software, hardware, middleware, and services from third parties that are used in conjunction with SAP solutions.

▶ **SAP user groups**
The focus and priorities of SAP development are strongly influenced by SAP user groups. These user group participants need to be centrally coordinated to ensure that the interests of the enterprise are purposefully represented in the SAP user groups.

5.6.3 Establishment Procedure

Organizational provisions regarding responsibilities are essential for establishing contract management. In this context, you must differentiate the roles of *contract manager* and *contract administrator*. Whereas the contract manager is responsible for contractual tasks, such as coordination and management of contracts with SAP, license fee agreements, transfer of system measurement information, as well as approval of installation releases, the contract administrator assumes responsibility for the operational SAP license management.

5.7 Coordination of Development Requests and Change Management

Experience has shown that most incidents that occur in the running SAP operation are the result of incorrect planning and implementation of changes. Unnecessary changes require considerable resources. Therefore, be sure to carefully check, plan, and control changes in the SAP solution landscape; make changes transparent; and ensure that the changes are implemented without affecting the running operation.

5.7.1 Goal of Change Management

Change management's goal is to efficiently and precisely implement changes to the SAP applications with minimal risks using standardized methods and procedures.

The implementation of this process has the following goals:

- **Careful use of resources**
  Particularly within the framework of change measures for optimization and continuously improvement, you must carefully check whether you can implement the required functionality, for example, by means of existing SAP solutions, for a new SAP release, a customer development, or a change request to SAP. Long-term service planning with defined maintenance dates forms the basis here.

- **Balance between necessity and effects**
  Each changes has benefits, results, and potential effects. These should be balanced with the costs for implementing the changes. You therefore must consider all organizational and technical dependencies as a whole and evaluate them by means of a cost efficiency analysis.

- **Minimizing the effects of changes**
  This target defines the central responsibility of change management to minimize the risks of failed changes or the consequences of changes by means of standardized methods and procedures. Therefore, decisions about changes must be made centrally by all units involved. This results in lower downtimes and increased user productivity.

- **Use of effective tools**
  All changes must be supported by suitable tools regardless of whether these changes concern business processes, implementation and upgrade projects, regular maintenance, or urgent corrections. The functions of SAP Solution Manager supports all critical phases of the SAP software lifecycle and enables you to process large amounts of changes in a plannable and secure manner.

▶ **Creation of transparency**
Effective change management becomes transparent by providing reports about the quality key figures and by establishing a targeted information policy for planned changes.

5.7.2 Responsibilities and Obligations

The change management process includes centrally coordinating enterprise development requests with SAP user groups, as well as coordinating changes within the SAP application support, such as enhancements, add-ons, modifications, and enterprise-internal developments. The following sections describe the two groups of changes based on SAP Solution Manager.

Controlling changes throughout the entire application lifecycle requires a close cooperation of the various groups and a coordinated schedule for the various change reasons, such as functions, maintenance, or problem solutions. Figure 5.7 shows the three main initiators for changes. Global or regional *business process champions* request the adaptation of solutions; *SAP* delivers new releases, support packages, and patches to maintain the solutions; and *users/key users* request the prevention of incidents.

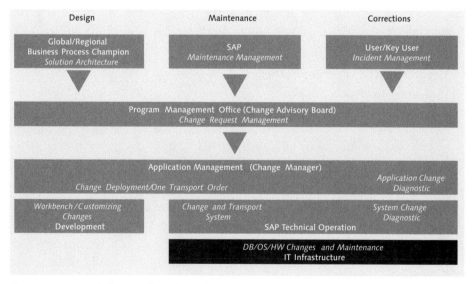

Figure 5.7 Control Changes Throughout the Entire Application Lifecycle

The Program Management Office is responsible for planning and scheduling the requested changes. To fulfill this task, Program Management Office should control the change request management process.

Basically, the application management team, the development team, and the SAP technical operations are responsible for the execution of the requested changes. The SAP Solution Manager function, *One Transport Order*, forms the basis for controlling the end-to-end software logistics beyond ABAP and the change deployment phase.

The application and system diagnostic of changes supports the customers in identifying, controlling, and verifying critical technical configurations, application configurations (e.g., customizing requests), and coding (e.g., ABAP workbench requests).

5.7.3 Establishment Procedure

To develop a change management for the application lifecycle, you need to define internal change processes within the enterprise in a transparent manner. Moreover, all necessary information concerning the SAP landscape must be available in a central system.

SAP recommends the following steps to implement this process:

1. Begin with *change diagnostics*, which supports customers in the identification, control, maintenance, and verification of different configuration versions of the SAP system landscape. This is the basis for change management of the application lifecycle.

2. *Change deployment* then provides a holistic overview of the application changes of a solution and should ensure that all involved components (ABAP and non-ABAP) of the application change are tested and released as a whole.

3. *Change request management* provides standardized methods and procedures to ensure an efficient and on-time implementation of the SAP software changes with minimal risks.

SAP Solution Manager is a preconfigured solution provided by SAP that is optimized to SAP-specific changes. You can find further details on this process and support information in the description of the SAP Standard, "Change Request Management and Change Control Management" (see *http://service.sap.com/supportstandards*).

5.8 Procedure for Developing the Process Model

Enterprise processes and IT and support organization processes have no departmental boundaries. Consequently, the path for a process and service organization must be implemented in a transparent, holistic strategy. Figure 5.8 shows such a logical path. The following sections describe the basic steps for developing the process implementation.

Figure 5.8 Process Implementation Procedure Model

5.8.1 Vision of Process Management

As in the CCC strategy development process, the starting point for establishing a process and service orientation is the definition of a vision for the process management. This vision provides the direction and targets of the implementation. It's essential that all people involved recognize the potential of comprehensive process optimization. This can be illustrated, for example, based on the implementation of cross-object and cross-departmental change processes. It can often be observed that the isolated implementation of change processes for defined objects (e.g., server infrastructures) only has a low optimization potential. The comprehensive approach, however, optimizes the used resources, for instance, by bundling the maintenance and associated test activities.

Through the creation of a process and service orientation, you can achieve the following:

▶ Create customer orientation

▶ Make decisions based on current process information

▶ Minimize operational risks

5.8.2 Process Model

The phase for defining a process model includes three basic steps:

1. Develop a process description methodology.

2. Develop a CCC process model.

3. Develop a CCC glossary.

To visualize the processes, you can use different models and tools. After you've defined the targets and requirements of the process model and the tools, you must determine the model and tool conventions. This convention must be communicated to the employees through training.

As already described, the CCC process model creates a joint, abstract, yet binding view of the CCC flow organization. The requirements of a process model can be defined as follows:

▶ Joint, binding view of the flow organization

▶ Presentation of all processes and their interactions

▶ Use of industry standards, for example, ITIL; these are only the tools for orientation and not the goal

▶ Providing suitable investment protection

The CCC glossary lists the terminology with conceptual, objective definitions required for understanding the CCC process model and to ensure the correct usage and unambiguous understanding of these technical terms. It has proven useful to use the original concepts of industry standards such as ITIL and to supplement them with enterprise and industry-specific terms.

5.8.3   Process Analysis

The systematic examination of the existing processes is supposed to detect weak points and improvement potentials. It's also a prerequisite to recognize process variants within the organization or within different configuration elements (e.g., servers, networks, applications) and to achieve a standardization and harmonization. The analysis typically includes the documentation of the current organizational situation and the subsequent as-is analysis of the processes. For this purpose, methods, such as assessments, benchmarks, and weak-point analysis, are used. The examination includes typical process criteria, for instance, process implementation, process effectiveness, process efficiency, and process interfaces. The determined weak points of the process analysis are documented in a structured manner and provide entry points for possible improvements.

5.8.4   Process Governance

The process governance defines the structures for two subject areas. It controls the responsibility for the process model and its further development, and the definition of the responsibility for the process implementation, the process result, the continuous monitoring and optimization of the CCC processes, as well as the mapping of the process responsibility in the current organization. To further develop the process model, you should create a permanent committee within the organization. This process board assumes the technical responsibility for the CCC process model and makes decisions for changes and the implementation of model improvements. The process board ensures a high acceptance of the processes by means of the following measures:

▶ Professional control and quality assurance of contents with regard to current projects

▶ Escalation if deviations have been identified

▶ Description, documentation, and publication in consistent form

▶ Methodological support of the process managers for describing, implementing, and developing the processes

The definition of interfaces and integration points of the process organization in the line organization is another task. Depending on the complexity of the organization, you must decide whether it's necessary and makes sense to separate the responsibility and implementation or control, and which further roles are necessary. You might find it reasonable to bundle responsibilities. For example, a process owner can be responsible for a set of processes, for example, all service support processes.

5.8.5   Process Projects

Processes and their weak points influence the CCC targets to different extents. This dependency should be mapped and considered for the definition and prioritization of the optimization projects. The prioritization is based on the criteria, *strategy*, *business case*, *resource availability*, and *risk*. Projects for process optimizations should be implemented gradually to avoid an overload of the organization. At the same time, you must consider current projects and line activities and align them with the program.

A defined sequence for the implementation of processes does not exist because the organizations are too different. However, you can achieve a considerably higher efficiency through the optimization of reactive processes, for example, incident, problem, and change management. The resources obtained through optimization can then be used for proactive processes, such as availability and capacity management. This leads to increased availability and risk minimization. Strategic processes require comparatively low resources and can and should be optimized anytime.

5.8.6   Process Operation

The processes are controlled and implemented based on key figures within the process operation.

5.8.7   Process Optimization

There are different models and methods for optimizing CCC processes. *Six Sigma* is one of the best known methods. Models, such as ITIL, SAP IT Service & Application Management [Schöler 05], and Standardized End-to-End Solution Operations [Active 07], define *what* is to be improved. Six Sigma, in contrast, delivers a procedure model for a structured optimization of the CCC processes; that is, it defines *how* you can achieve these improvements.

In this context, you can use a structured procedure model that implements the process improvement in five phases: *Define – Measure – Analyze – Improve – Control* (DMAIC). These phases are implemented one after the other using tools and methods to deliver defined results. Figure 5.9 shows the phases of the DMAIC cycle.

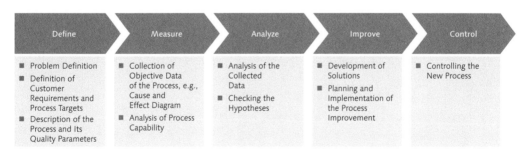

Figure 5.9   DMAIC Cycle

If the knowledge about the methods and tools of Six Sigma is available within the enterprise, you can use them to support selected CCC processes.

For example, you can use the methods, *CTQ* (Critical to Quality – a method for describing the quality-defining, critical parameters of a process) and *Voc* (Voice of the Customer – a method for obtaining concrete target figures from a verbal customer problem to eliminate a problem), to structure the implementation process of SLAs.

5.9   Summary

The process model is the backbone of your SAP CCC. A process model that is based on the latest version of ITIL serves as a reference. In addition, you are provided with SAP standards for the application operation (SAP Standards for Solution Operations), which you can use to achieve a high process quality. The establishment of the SLM, the processes relevant for SAP certification (Service Desk and incident management, information management, contract management), and the administration of development requests, are all essential for the smooth operation of your SAP CCC.

6 Architecture Management and SAP Solution Manager

Like the business-oriented CCC strategy, governance, and comprehensive process model, efficient architecture management for the SAP solutions assumes a critical role in the enterprise for successfully setting up and enhancing SAP CCC.

This chapter therefore introduces architecture management as well as SAP Solution Manager as the central component for implementing and operating SAP solutions. This includes the future development strategy, new functions, and the implementation procedure.

The last section discusses the Value Assessment for SAP Solution Manager service, which provides a methodical procedure to identify, evaluate, and aggregate the benefit potentials of SAP Solution Manager.

6.1 Architecture Management

The architecture concept describes the main components of a system and their relationships. For example, software architecture refers to a structured or hierarchical arrangement of the system components as well as to the description of their relationships [Balzert 01].

In the context of SAP CCC, three different architectures are relevant: the *business process architecture*, the *application architecture*, and the *technical system architecture* (see Figure 6.1):

▶ **Business process architecture**
This architecture indicates which business processes exist in an enterprise; how individual business processes consist of main processes, subprocesses, and activities; and how the business processes are related, that is, which process output is the input for another process at the same time.

▶ **Application architecture**
In conjunction with SAP CCC, this architecture doesn't refer to the internal architecture of individual application systems (e.g., SAP ERP and SAP CRM) but comprises all SAP application systems and their relationships to each other and to non-SAP systems. Moreover, the application architecture indicates which systems are used to support specific business processes. In the following sections, the architecture of integration platforms and so-called application server and Basis systems is considered part of the application architecture.

▶ **Technical architecture**
This architecture basically describes the infrastructure components that you need to run the application systems. These include, for example, the components of the physical network, the operating systems, and the database management systems (DBMSs).

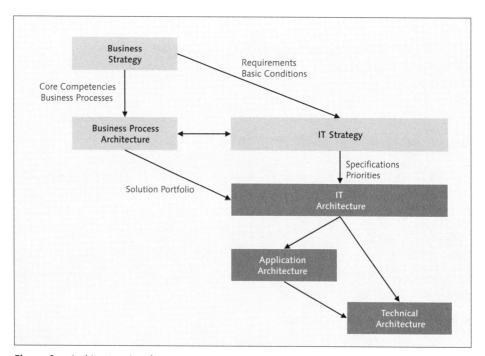

Figure 6.1 Architecture Levels

The tasks of SAP CCC mainly concern the application architecture in enterprises because this is where SAP solutions are used. However, because you must derive the application architecture from the business process architecture, you also need to understand the latter. This is also indicated by the fact that business process knowledge is considered a critical competence of SAP CCC in real-world scenarios (see Section 2.5).

SAP provides *solution maps* for the coordination with the user department. They represent industry-specific references for business process architectures and help you form a holistic understanding of the business processes that are supposed to be supported. Figure 6.2 shows the SAP solution map for insurances as an example, which can also be found on the SAP Service Marketplace (*http://service.sap.com/BMET*).

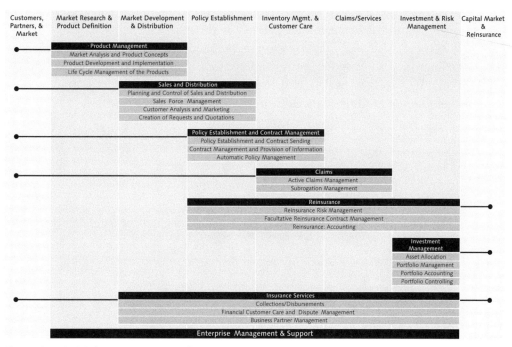

Figure 6.2 SAP Solution Map – Example: Insurances

In architecture management, it's particularly essential to distinguish between the *actual architecture* and the *target architecture*.

You need a clear understanding of how the current business process architecture and the existing application architecture are structured to be able to design the target architecture for your application systems on the basis of the target architecture for the business processes.

For a step-by-step transition from the actual to the planned architecture, you need a *phase plan*, which provides information on the schedule and the SAP application systems you want to use to support specific business processes. This phase plan is often called the *development plan* in real-world situations.

The development plan specifies the CCC strategy (see Chapter 3) and must be complemented by a detailed migration plan that defines which application may have to be replaced and which data should be migrated to the new systems.

6.2 Architecture Standards

Architecture management isn't possible without architecture standards. Because the development plan, that is, the transformation from the actual to the planned architecture, is a long-term process, you need binding specifications for application system classes but also for specific technical systems at the infrastructure level. These standards must be included in the IT or CCC strategy.

To comply with the standards, easy and transparent communication is required. Figure 6.3 shows a proposal that enables you to structure and easily communicate the main standards at the application and technical levels.

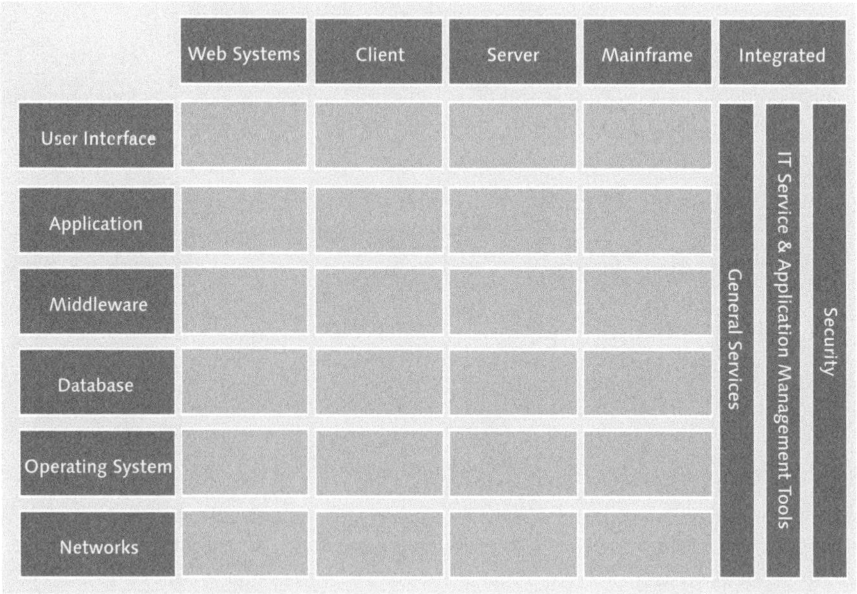

Figure 6.3 Structuring Proposal for Architecture Standards

For single system standards in the overall architecture, you can use the template to navigate to the next level (see Figure 6.4).

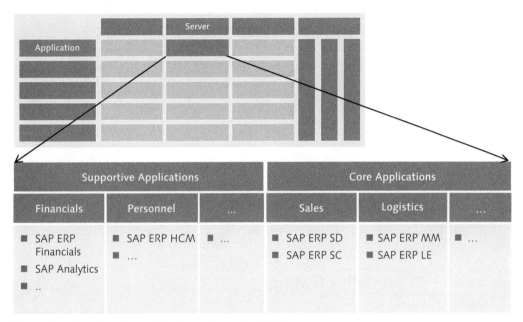

Figure 6.4 Structure Proposal for Second-Level Applications

This presentation considers elements of the application architecture and technical architecture as well as cross-sections of subjects, such as tools for IT service and application management. This includes, for example, software systems for incident management, change management, problem management, configuration management, monitoring, and job control. Such tools are critical because they directly affect the efficiency of your CCC organization.

You should describe all elements on the basis of standardized descriptive elements, such as category, class, and area of application. Table 6.1 illustrates this rule with an example.

This table provides an overview of all currently used products, the target landscape, and planned migration dates.

Descriptive Element	Definition	Example
Category	► Grouping of functionally related elements	► IT service and application management processes
Class	► Structure level below a category	► Change management
Area of application	► Area of application of the standard	► All companies
Actual standards	► Currently defined standard	► Customer development
Actual products	► Currently used products	► Change Manager 3.1
Planned standards	► Planned future standards	► Standard software
Planned products	► Planned future products	► SAP Solution Manager
Migration date	► Date for the migration to the planned product	► 200x

Table 6.1 Architecture of the Descriptive Elements

6.3 SAP Solution Manager

SAP Solution Manager is the central platform for the implementation and operation of SAP solutions and thus enables the collaboration of all parties involved in the SAP operation, such as SAP CCC, sourcing partners, external consultant partners, and SAP support organizations. At the same time, SAP Solution Manager promotes the efficiency of the management of existing application systems and supports you in implementing the development plan for your application architecture. Consequently, SAP Solution Manager is a mandatory tool for SAP CCC.

SAP Solution Manager is based on five main concepts:

► **Business process orientation**
IT isn't just used as an end in itself but supports the business areas with process-supporting IT services.

► **Support of the entire lifecycle of SAP solutions**
The support of the entire lifecycle of SAP solutions minimizes frictional losses at the interfaces between the different lifecycle phases, from the introduction, to the operational operation, to the continuous optimization. In all phases, you are provided with a uniform information basis.

▶ **Holistic view of the solution**

Individual business processes are often supported by numerous SAP and non-SAP solutions. The failure risk of the process support, particularly for changes, can only be minimized by the comprehensive consideration of all interfaces and relationships.

▶ **Openness**

Openness means that non-SAP products are also supported by the functions of SAP Solution Manager.

▶ **Governance**

SAP Solution Manager supports the governance of the processes for the IT service and application management by means of central planning, control, and monitoring.

SAP Solution Manager (SAP PRESS, 2006) provides a comprehensive overview of the functions of SAP Solution Manager. At this point, we focus on the enhancements.

The current version of SAP Solution Managers 4.0 is further developed according to the strategy illustrated in Figure 6.5.

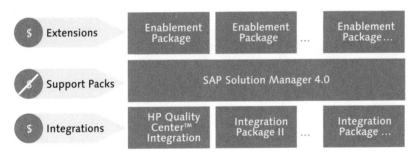

Figure 6.5 SAP Solution Manager: Strategy

Free-of-charge *support packs* are provided on an ongoing basis. They serve to improve already existing functions.

You can also gradually extend the functions of SAP Solution Manager with so-called *enablement packages*. They include extended functions for specific target groups.

Finally, *integration packages* enable you to easily and quickly integrate third-party tools (e.g., HP Quality Center).

6.3.1 Standard Scenarios

SAP Solution Manager supports *end-to-end support* in all phases of the lifecycle of IT solutions. Figure 6.6 maps the SAP Solution Manager standard scenarios to the individual lifecycle phases.

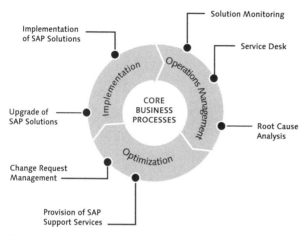

Figure 6.6 Standard Scenarios of SAP Solution Manager

The following list describes the standard scenarios of SAP Solution Manager:

▸ **Implementation and upgrade of SAP solutions**
In the context of implementation projects and upgrades, SAP Solution Manager supports methods and tools for user training, use of best practices for project management, and access to SAP specialist knowledge by means of an integrated test suite, for example.

▸ **Solution monitoring**
SAP Solution Manager provides a high level of automation for the SAP application operation, particularly central business process and system monitoring as well as notifications when errors occur. Moreover, you can collect data from the used alert monitors for defined periods and analyze and valuate it automatically via early watch alerts or for specific customers via business intelligence methods. Such reports support service level reporting.

▸ **Service desk**
The SAP Solution Manager service desk is a preconfigured trouble ticket system that allows efficient management of and solutions for problem reports.

▶ **Root cause analysis**
SAP Solution Manager diagnostics enable an efficient and secure root cause analysis of incidents in IT solutions by means of standardized procedures and a uniform user interface. BMC Appsight and CA Wily Introscope are integral components of the end-to-end root cause analysis. BMC Appsight for Windows/.NET enables an end-to-end root cause analysis up to the user desktop by monitoring the user activities. CA Wily Introscope provides support for analyzing server performance problems. In this context, the system collects server data and transfers it to SAP Solution Manager.

▶ **Delivery of SAP support services**
SAP Solution Manager is the platform that you can use to request and document SAP support services. Results, reports, and found issues are provided in SAP Solution Manager for all cooperating parties and can be tracked there. It thus serves as a central information store.

▶ **Change request management**
SAP Solution Manager provides workflow-based, completely documented support for the *change management*, *project management*, and *change logistics* processes (particularly transport system). Due to the integration of the change and transport system (CTS), which can be extended with the option to transport Java objects, you can directly transport objects from change request management.

6.3.2 New Standard Functions

SAP Solution Manager offers the following new standard functions:

▶ **SAP Solution Manager Maintenance Optimizer**
This function allows for a completely preconfigured maintenance management process. This facilitates the entire change management process and also increases transparency, which improves control and controlling processes.

▶ **One Transport Order (OTO)**
As already mentioned, SAP Solution Manager 4.0 (Support Package 12) enables you to use the transport option of CTS for Java objects. This considerably reduces the effort required to synchronize changes in mixed landscapes (ABAP + Java).

▶ **Change control management**
Change control management records significant configuration changes, for example, critical changes at the database, operating system, Java, or ABAP level

in their history, which enables you to compare and analyze them across the entire landscape. Thus, it's possible to identify changes in a system landscape within a period as causes of incidents.

6.3.3 Enablement Packages

Enablement packages are support tools that enable you to perform specific tasks more efficiently. The following sections provide a selection of available packages.

The *solution support enablement package* delivers tools for managing upgrades, testing the application, consolidating the system, and reverse business engineering:

- ▶ **SAP Reverse Business Engineer** facilitates the analysis of live SAP systems and the selection of business process data as well as its use in the corresponding SAP systems.

- ▶ **SAP Test Data Migration Server** supports you in creating small, manageable test environments with consistent and relevant business process data.

- ▶ **SAP Custom Development Optimization Package** improves the analysis of customer-specific developments and their effects with regard to upgrades or changes.

- ▶ To improve the **root cause analysis** for non-SAP systems, you can use the enhanced scope of the BMC Appsight for Windows/.NET and CA Wily Introscope products.

- ▶ **Service Desk Extended Usage** extends the usage of the standard service desks in SAP Solution Manager to the management of all problems regarding IT and telecommunication devices.

For an up-to-date overview and detailed information refer to *http://service.sap.com/sep*.

6.3.4 Integration Packages

The *integration packages* by SAP enable you to integrate existing best-of-breed tools on the side of the customer and consequently to protect existing investments. The following list introduces two examples of this approach:

- ▶ **HP Quality Center**
  The integration of the HP tool extends the test options of SAP Solution Manager and thus helps you reduce risks, minimize test cycles, and save costs.

▶ **Redwood Cronacle**

Because solution landscapes become more and more complex and heterogeneous, you also need cross-landscape job management. SAP meets this requirement by allowing for an integration of the job scheduling tool, Cronacle, by Redwood with SAP NetWeaver. Due to the complete integration, the landscape-wide planning, monitoring, and evaluation, particularly of job chains, are considerably extended.

6.3.5 Role-Based Process Support in SAP Solution Manager

SAP Solution Manager consistently supports the concept of role-based specialization of the organization, which has been introduced in conjunction with the SAP model for the SAP application operation (see Section 4.3). SAP end-to-end standards are embedded in role-based work centers that bundle workflows, Web-based inboxes, launch pads, and so on. Consequently, the role carriers can access all standard processes or process steps in which they are involved from a central location (see Figure 6.7).

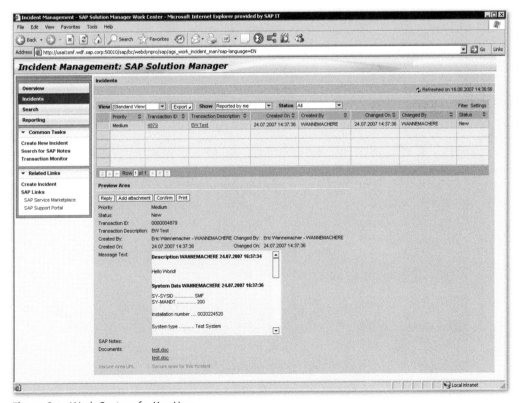

Figure 6.7 Work Center of a Key User

The work center shown in the figure enables the *key user* role to centrally access all processes in which the key user is involved. This includes, for example, the *incident management, change control management, exception handling,* and *upgrade* process standards. Within the processes, the key user can carry out single steps, for example, new incidents. Meaningful reports support your daily work.

6.4 Implementation of SAP Solution Manager

You shouldn't implement SAP Solution Manager without planning. Consequently, you must orient toward the CCC strategy that you pursue in your enterprise (see Chapter 3).

SAP thus recommends the implementation procedure shown in Figure 6.8. This procedure both helps you avoid the risks in the operational operation and maximizes the sustainability of the use of SAP Solution Manager and your CCC organization.

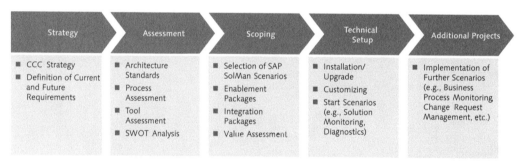

Figure 6.8 SAP Solution Manager Roadmap

SAP supports this roadmap by numerous standardized services, for example, SAP Solution Manager scoping workshop, starter packs for the implementation of individual functions, or the value assessment for SAP Solution Manager.

6.5 Value Assessment for SAP Solution Manager

Like the implementation of an application system, in most enterprises, the decision to use SAP Solution Manager is also based on the results of a cost efficiency analysis. This analysis compares the benefit potentials from the usage to the costs for the implementation and operation.

SAP provides the *value assessment for SAP Solution Manager* to help you methodically identify, valuate, and aggregate the benefit potentials.

You valuate the individual potentials by comparing the specific business situation with benchmarks from other real-world projects.

Figure 6.9 shows the main benefit potentials with the dimensions of the total cost of ownership (TCO). The use of SAP Solution Manager particularly leads to a reduction of the IT costs for the implementation and enhancement of SAP solutions.

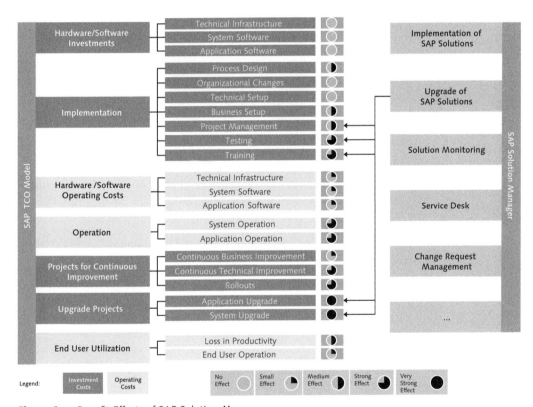

Figure 6.9 Benefit Effects of SAP Solution Manager

In addition to these measurable benefit potentials, the use of SAP Solution Manager provides further benefits for your enterprise, for example:

▶ Use of SAP best practices in industry-specific business processes

▶ Promotion of the harmonization and standardization of the business process architecture and application architecture

The costs that you will incur when using SAP Solution Manager depend on the specific business situation and thus need to be determined individually for each case.

By comparing the benefit potentials with the costs for the initial investment and running operation, you can determine the economic benefits of using SAP Solution Manager via established mathematical financial procedures (e.g., net present value calculation).

6.6 Summary

Managing the architecture of SAP solutions in the enterprise is a central task of SAP CCC. To reduce complexity, you should distinguish between the different architecture levels, such as *business processes*, *application systems*, and *infrastructure systems*. Architecture standards assist you in transferring the strategic goals of SAP CCC to the architecture of the SAP solutions.

SAP Solution Manager supports you in managing the architectures. SAP provides an established procedure, the value assessment, to identify and valuate the benefit potentials to determine how you can use the central platform for the implementation and operation of your SAP solutions most efficiently.

7   Competences and Qualification for the CCC Organization

Employee creativity, motivation, and competence are critical competitive factors for enterprises. To enable SAP CCC to develop qualification planning that is oriented toward the objectives of the enterprise, you need to know the future requirements for the employees.

This chapter provides an overview of future key qualifications of the CCC employees and instructions to plan the qualification. It also names relevant training methods and introduces the SAP Learning Solution — a tool that supports all relevant training processes in your enterprise.

7.1   Key Qualifications

Today's IT organizations face numerous structure problems:

▸ Employees are predominantly middle-aged and older.

▸ Employees are trained for technologies and systems that are rarely used.

▸ Employees have limited process and business knowledge.

As a result of these structure problems, the organization may no longer be able to meet the requirements.

To perform future strategic, conceptual, and realistic tasks with the necessary service orientation, you require a new category of IT managers and IT employees. In this context, Gartner has coined the term *versatilist* [Morello 05]. Versatilists are employees that add value to the enterprise with a combination of specialization and generalization.

Figure 7.1 illustrates the characteristics of the different competences of specialists, generalists, and versatilists. However, it's questionable whether each employee of the IT organization must follow this model. Still, it's a fact that IT employees already face a lot of changes, which will even increase in the next years.

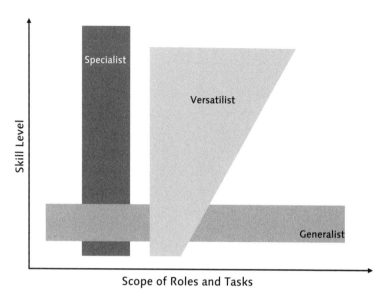

Figure 7.1 Specialist, Generalist, Versatilist

Due to future requirements, it's generally assumed that CCC employees will specialize in one of the following four areas: business process management, technology management, knowledge management, and collaboration and sourcing management (see Figure 7.2).

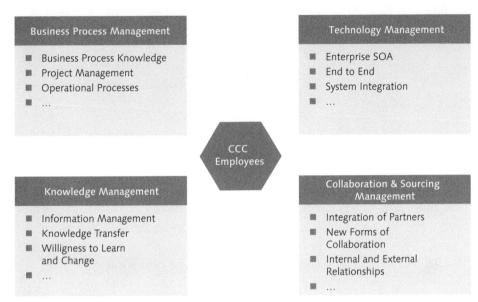

Figure 7.2 Future Specializations of CCC Employees

The increasing availability, performance, data integrity, and other requirements of business areas in SAP solutions require comprehensive knowledge of the technologies used and their relationships to each other. This knowledge will remain the core of functioning CCC organizations in the future.

Furthermore, CCC organizations need employees that are able to optimize and implement end-to-end business processes in coordination with the business areas. Consequently, the knowledge about the business process should be enhanced. This is the only way to enable IT to support these processes in an effective way as well as identify dependencies and quickly provide the appropriate solution in case of failures.

Both implementing and operating SAP solutions are not possible without partners of the CCC ecosystem. You're supposed to integrate technology partners, service providers, or SAP with the CCC processes as smoothly as possible, which requires you to implement and operate new forms of collaboration and sourcing. This, in turn, requires CCC employees that work integratively.

Due to the flow of information, the targeted, role-based provision of up-to-date information in the SAP environment and the active knowledge transfer will become an increasing problem. Consequently, you need to establish competences to control the knowledge management process.

You need to specifically qualify your employees based on previously defined, general future performance requirements and enterprise-specific requirements that can be derived from the CCC strategy.

7.2 Qualification

The individual educational planning for the employees should always be based on medium-term, cross-CCC resource planning, which should rely on roles according to the SAP Standards for Solution Operations. After determining the number of necessary capacities for the individual roles, you plan the training for each role. In this process, SAP supports you with qualification and certification offers that are based on the reference processes of the SAP Standards for Solution Operations. Some examples of these are provided in Table 7.1. You can find more detailed information and training dates at *www.sap.com/education*.

Certified Role	End-to-End Training
Program manager	Managing End-to-End Solution Operations
	Technical Upgrade Management
Application management expert	Root Cause Analysis
	Change Control Management
Business process expert	Business Process Integration and Automation Management
SAP technical administrator	SAP NetWeaver Application Server
	Java Administration

Table 7.1 Certified Roles and Training

For the selection of the training offers, you should use a *blended-learning approach*, that is, combine the benefits of classroom training with those of e-learning.

Figure 7.3 shows the range of blended-learning approaches with the possible combinations of learning methods, media, and orientation toward learning theory [Wiepcke 06].

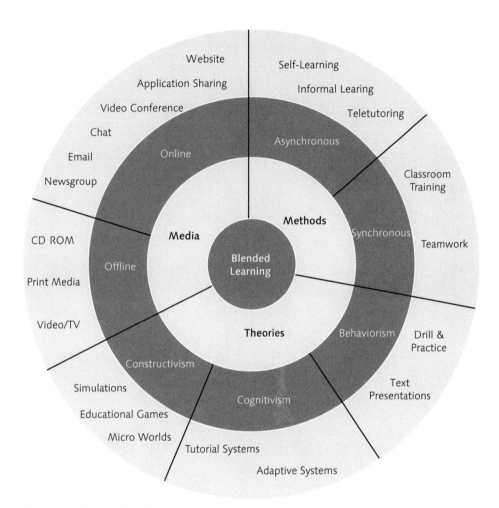

Figure 7.3 Blended-Learning Approach

You should plan the entire education completely on the basis of roles. Against the background of decreasing budgets, this prevents faulty investments. However, this approach enables you to draft the requirements for external employees by means of uniform educational planning.

As illustrated in Figure 7.4, educational planning should consider all identified necessary key qualifications. Besides technical training (*skill*), you should also include training that communicates soft skills (*will*).

	1st Level	2nd Level	3rd Level	Course Title	Course Code	Key User	Appl. Mgmt.	Developer	...
	SAP ERP	Analytics	SEM	Strategic Enterprise Management	SEM010	O	O	O	O
	SAP ERP	Analytics	...		...	N	N	N	N
	SAP ERP	Financials	Financial Accounting	SAP ERP Financials Overview	SAPFIN				
	...	...							
Skill	IT Service Management	Basic Principles		ITIL Foundation Course	ITIL01		X		
	...								
	E2E Solution Operation	Technical Core Competence		E2E Root Cause Analysis	E2E100		X		
	E2E Solution Operation	Technical Expert Competence		E2E Change Control Management	E2E200				
	...								
	Customer Orientation	Basic Principles		Customer Orientation Basic Principles	KO01				
Will	...								
	Self Management	Target and Time Management		Target and Time Management	ZZ01	X			
	...								

Legend: N = Necessary; O = Optional

Figure 7.4 Educational Planning

You can then create individual training plans for the respective roles. These can be centrally provided to all CCC employees, including all relevant course information, such as duration, content, and dates, as illustrated in the following customer example (Figure 7.5).

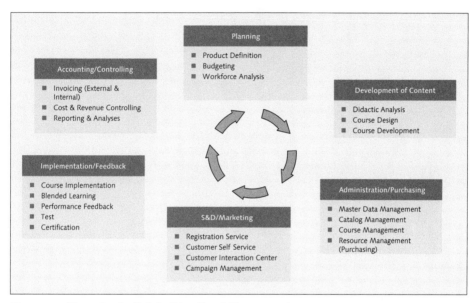

Figure 7.5 Elements of a Holistic Educational Management

Subsequently, you link the role-based educational planning with the concrete planning for the individual employees. You should provide the information on completed qualifications centrally because this information may be useful when selecting the appropriate employees, for example, for SAP implementation projects.

7.3 SAP Learning Solution

If the processes for holistic training and skill enhancement management haven't been efficiently defined in your enterprise, you should support these processes with an integrated tool solution, particularly in large customer organizations. These solutions should cover the areas illustrated in Figure 7.6 and allow for options to integrate special solutions, for example, Web Based Training (WBT).

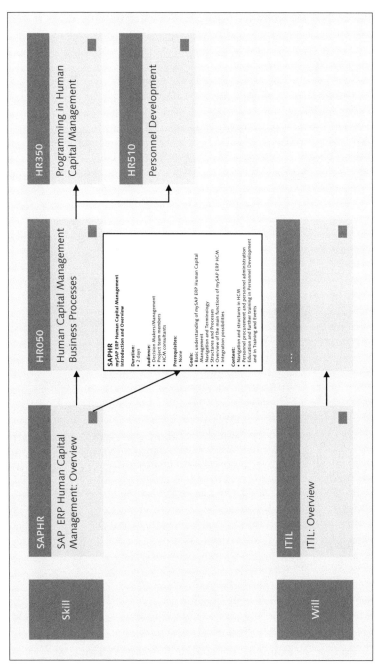

Figure 7.6 Learning Map

The CCC organization may benefit from the implementation of such a solution with regard to the support in user training, for example, in conjunction with implementation projects, as well as in its own CCC organization.

SAP Learning Solution (Figure 7.7) is a tool used for holistic training and skill enhancement management.

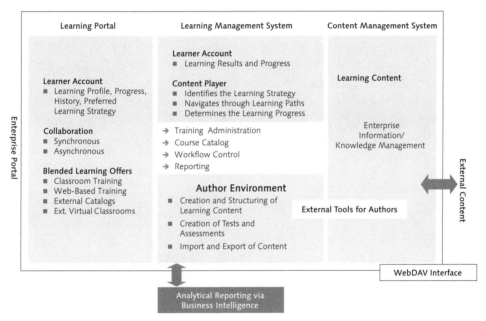

Figure 7.7 SAP Learning Solution

The solution shown in Figure 7.7 has a modular structure with the following characteristics:

▸ Covers all relevant educational processes in enterprises of all sizes and industries

▸ Links the learning processes with the business processes via complete integration with SAP ERP

▸ Provides predefined roles for all stakeholders (students, trainers, authors, managers, controlling, and so on)

▸ Enables key performance indicator-driven controlling and the control of the educational processes via a score card

▸ Enables the evaluation of the learning progress of teams

▸ Has an open architecture (SAP NetWeaver)

7.4 Summary

With new requirements for enterprises regarding the flexibility of business processes and a global market presence, the requirements for the qualifications of CCC employees change, too. For example, you can determine an increasing significance of so-called versatilists that are able to process very different issues. Furthermore, you must take individual qualification measures for the individual roles in SAP CCC (e.g., program manager or business process expert). Here, you can use approaches that combine different learning types (e.g., classroom trainings or e-learning offers). Finally, SAP Learning Solution is a powerful tool to plan and control your educational planning.

8 Procedure for Establishing SAP CCC

For establishing SAP CCC, you must first identify the initial situation for the fields of activity described in the previous chapters. You can use the *CCC maturity model* for this purpose. Based on this estimate, you develop a *roadmap* in the second step. You must ensure that the roadmap is conducted through suitable measures of organizational change management.

8.1 CCC Maturity Degree

The CCC maturity model illustrated in Figure 8.1 supports you in the identification of the initial situation and the current degree of maturity of the IT organization with regard to the CCC fields of activity.

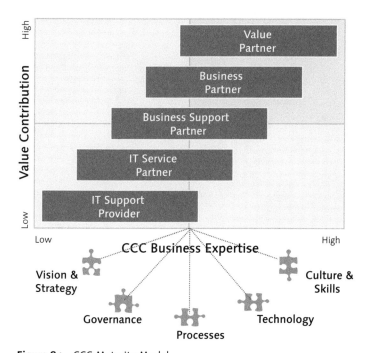

Figure 8.1 CCC Maturity Model

The model relates the technical expertise of SAP CCC to its value contribution. The more precise the understanding of the business processes, the higher the added value for the enterprise success.

In this context, you must distinguish five different degrees of maturity that range from *IT support provider* to *value partner*. The last level does not constitute the optimal degree of maturity for all enterprises. The degree of maturity to be strived for depends on the significance of IT for the enterprise.

If IT services contribute considerably to the added value of an enterprise (e.g., in the banking segment), SAP CCC requires an extensive understanding of the technical requirements and the business processes of the enterprise and should be developed as a value partner.

The *strategy matrix* shown in Figure 8.2 (according to [Nolan 05]) supports you in defining the role of the overall IT function.

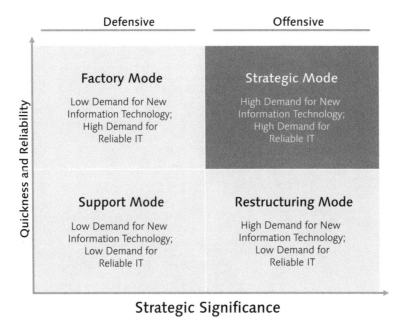

Figure 8.2 Role of IT for Enterprise Success

The CCC organization must be aligned with the assignment of the IT function to the respective quadrants. Based on this assignment, you then must attain the appropriate degree of maturity. An enterprise, in which IT is the decisive innovative factor, strives for a high degree of maturity for its CCC organization.

The characteristics of the individual degrees of maturity, which are listed in Table 8.1, help you determine the appropriate maturity degree.

Maturity Degree	Field of Activity	Characteristics
IT support provider	▸ Strategy ▸ Governance ▸ Processes ▸ Technology ▸ Culture and skills	▸ Vision and strategy not defined ▸ Control via IT costs, focus on IT operation ▸ Processes not defined ▸ Isolated decisions for tools ▸ Focus on IT skills
IT service partner	▸ Strategy ▸ Governance ▸ Processes ▸ Technology ▸ Culture and skills	▸ CCC strategy derived from IT goals ▸ Control via IT-focused KPIs ▸ Compliance with the minimum criteria of CCC certification ▸ Mutual decision on the selection ▸ Service orientation, SAP solution knowledge
Business support partner	▸ Strategy ▸ Governance ▸ Processes ▸ Technology ▸ Culture and skills	▸ CCC strategy developed in cooperation with IT management ▸ Control via measurable service levels ▸ Established role-based process organization ▸ Defined standards, SLA reporting ▸ Customer focus
Business partner	▸ Strategy ▸ Governance ▸ Processes ▸ Technology ▸ Culture and skills	▸ CCC strategy derived from enterprise goals ▸ Decisions based on technical specifications ▸ Alignment with business process model ▸ Integration of business processes and tools Business process, enterprise SOA, and integration expertise

Table 8.1 Characteristics of CCC Maturity Degrees

Maturity Degree	Field of Activity	Characteristics
Value partner	▶ Strategy ▶ Governance ▶ Processes ▶ Technology ▶ Culture and skills	▶ Strategy as a business enabler ▶ Control based on value contribution for the enterprise ▶ Holistic service management lifecycle ▶ End-to-end control of business processes ▶ Value orientation, continuous improvements

Table 8.1 Characteristics of CCC Maturity Degrees (Cont.)

8.2 Developing the Roadmap

SAP provides a detailed reference roadmap (see Table 8.2) that is subdivided into the *initiation*, *planning*, *implementation*, *monitoring*, and *controlling* phases (see also *http://service.sap.com/cccnet*).

Phase	Result
Initiation	
CCC vision and CCC strategy	▶ CCC vision is defined and communicated ▶ CCC strategy is integrated with business and IT strategy ▶ Future CCC functions are defined and assigned to the organizational units ▶ Key success factors are defined
Organization	▶ Plan is defined (business case), and program responsibilities are determined ▶ Structure and flow organization are defined ▶ Necessary resources are defined ▶ Initial roadmap is developed ▶ Infrastructure is provided
Kickoff	▶ Kickoff event is implemented ▶ Teams are created ▶ Training of teams is completed (e.g., ITIL)

Table 8.2 CCC Roadmap

Phase	Result
Planning	
Assessments	▶ CCC assessments are implemented (maturity degree of CCC organization in the dimensions of the CCC fields of activity)
	▶ Service reporting is analyzed
	▶ Customer requirements are specified
	▶ Customer satisfaction survey is completed
	▶ CCC cost analysis is completed
	▶ SAP application and system landscape is evaluated
Service strategy	▶ CCC customers are defined
	▶ Service portfolio and services are defined
	▶ CCC resource requirement is defined
	▶ Sourcing alternatives are evaluated, and sourcing strategy is defined
CCC governance	▶ CCC organizational structure is defined
	▶ CCC governance dimensions are defined (e.g., committees)
	▶ CCC services and KPI reporting are defined
	▶ Risk management processes are defined
	▶ CCC resources are defined
CCC processes	▶ CCC process model is developed
	▶ CCC processes, functions, and roles are defined
CCC technology	▶ System management technologies are defined (e.g., SAP Solution Manager for test management)
	▶ Concepts for managing SAP technologies are developed (e.g., monitoring, administration, job control, etc.)
CCC Culture and skills	▶ Change management concept is developed
	▶ Training concept is defined

Table 8.2 CCC Roadmap (Cont.)

Phase	Result
Implementation, monitoring, controlling	
CCC governance	▸ Required committees are established
	▸ Governance dimensions are developed
CCC processes	▸ CCC process model is established
	▸ CCC processes are implemented with prioritization
	▸ Processes are continuously optimized
CCC technology	▸ Technologies are established to support CCC processes (see SAP Solution Manager Roadmap in Section 6.4)
CCC culture and skills	▸ Ensuring the necessary qualifications of CCC employees (skill/will)

Table 8.2 CCC Roadmap (Cont.)

8.3 Organizational Change Management

Setting up and optimizing SAP CCC is associated with numerous changes for the employees involved. To achieve the CCC targets, this change process must be conducted by means of suitable measures of organizational change management.

SAP has analyzed a large number of projects and identified six key success factors for change management. These success factors should not be taken as being optional but rather complement and build on each other.

▸ **First success factor: Creating a Common Orientation**
The goals that are associated with setting up or further developing SAP CCC must be codified, visualized in a requirements-oriented way, and communicated to all employees in the appropriate target groups. The improvement to the level of information and the orientation toward the change objectives allow a joint orientation that in turn can represent a prerequisite for a greater preparedness to accept change.

▸ **Second success factor: Generating Conviction**
Knowledge of the changes in SAP CCC and the related goals alone isn't sufficient to ensure that employees will lend their support to it. Employees must be convinced of the necessity for the changes, must know what benefits the new orientation will bring, and must accept those benefits. In addition, they must know that the top management, as well as their line managers, supports

this plan and the associated changes. In this context, the principle that "to be affected is to get involved" should be taken to heart. As many employees as possible must actively be considered in the changes. This transforms fears into security, enables practical solutions to be found, and maximizes the motivation levels of all involved.

▶ **Third success factor: Ensuring Competence**
Employees preparedness for change and ability to change aren't the only factors that affect the success of the change process. The employees must also be properly qualified to put them in a position to use the new processes and solutions effectively. This is necessary to bring the knowledge to the employees effectively and efficiently and optimize the overall costs.

▶ **Fourth success factor: Ensuring a Uniform Perception**
The employees responsible for implementing the changes have an important communication and multiplication function for the project. The more consistent their behavior and their communication toward the employees affected, the easier a common orientation can be reached and conviction can be established. Define clear communication guidelines and draw on established communication channels.

▶ **Fifth success factor: Making Results Tangible**
When an implementation begins, the changes are not yet tangible. Frequently, the employees affected lack a concrete perception of the new developments. With this in mind, it's important to make results visible and tangible as early as possible. Open information seminars have proven useful here. These are intended to provide the option of learning about the benefits of the new organization, processes, and technologies; to get informed about the progress of the activities; and to address existing fears.

▶ **Sixth success factor: Safeguarding the Sustainability of Changes**
Change processes will only remain successful in the longer term if the new ways of thinking and acting are positively strengthened, and if employees are encouraged to live out the desired changes and help to shape and develop the change within sensible boundaries.

An important point here is the ongoing organizational mapping of the structures required. This can include a forum that evaluates the suggestions for improvement and decides on their implementation.

8.4 Summary

When setting up and developing SAP CCC, it's important to initially determine the starting point. For this purpose, you can use the CCC maturity model that compares the value contribution of SAP CCC with the technical expertise. Based on the maturity degree, you can derive a roadmap that you can use to obtain your strategic CCC targets. Because the flows and practices of the employees usually change, you should implement the appropriate measures of organizational change management. The central success factors are described within the scope of this book.

9 SAP Services for the CCC Organization

SAP is aware of the challenges for the SAP solution operation in enterprises and wants to face these challenges together with the enterprises. For this reason, the SAP service offer is continuously checked, adapted, and enhanced. By means of the SAP Standards for Solution Operations as well as the new functions of SAP Solution Manager that are discussed in this book, you can optimize the IT support organization to sustainably support the added value strategy of your enterprise.

The SAP CCC service portfolio, which is described in this chapter, provides comprehensive services and professional consulting services for setting up and optimizing your CCC organization.

You can find the complete SAP service portfolio at *www.sap.com/services/portfolio/index.epx*. For more information on the various services refer to *SAP Service and Support* (SAP PRESS, 2006).

9.1 CCC Community

SAP CCC can revert to a large and established community to compile and exchange knowledge for SAP solutions. This community includes SAP customers, SAP partners, and SAP. The user groups are independent interest groups of SAP users and play a significant role. They've made it their business "to create customized SAP solutions by controlling the functional enhancement and improvement of SAP products according to the users' requirements" (see *www.asug.com*).

The *International Competence Center Community* (ICCC) is an international umbrella organization for the cooperation of SAP CCCs and SAP. This organization combines several national organizations, among others, *Americas' SAP Users' Group* (ASUG) and *German-Speaking SAP User Group* (DSAG).

Within the SAP user groups, the CCC work groups comprise the largest number of members, which demonstrates the significance of the service and support topics. The collaboration in this strong community enables knowledge interchange, as well as bundling user interests toward SAP.

SAP promotes collaboration with user groups at various levels. Strategic topics and long-term planning for further developments of SAP solutions and services are discussed during meetings of various executive boards and at special forums. Work groups as well as special task forces develop requirements and solutions for operational subjects. Information about current topics is communicated through special profiles, for example, theme days, workshops, and webcasts.

We recommend that all SAP CCCs actively participate in the respective national user groups, contribute to the community, and represent the interests of the enterprise.

9.2 SAP CCC Service Portfolio

SAP provides holistic CCC consulting services to its customers. As shown in Figure 9.1, these services were assigned to the phases of an IT solution lifecycle (*planning, building, running*).

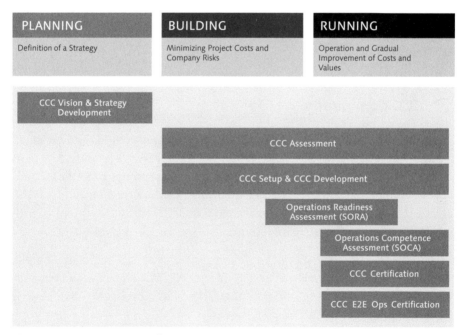

Figure 9.1 SAP CCC Service Offer

The tables in the following section briefly describe the challenges, benefits, and results of the offered services.

9.2.1 CCC Vision and Strategy Development

In cooperation with the enterprise, SAP develops an objective of the tasks to be fulfilled by SAP CCC and how SAP CCC will be positioned within the enterprise. Then, this vision is specified as a strategy. The enterprise is provided with key figures that can be used to evaluate the optimization of the support organization and promote it based on the results.

Challenges	Benefits	Results
► (New) orientation of the CCC activities toward enterprise and IT strategy ► Proof for strategic value contribution of SAP CCC for the enterprise ► Development of a CCC strategy	► Joint analysis of enterprise and IT strategy ► Transfer of industry best practices ► Development of a replicable strategy planning process	► Documented and communicated CCC vision and CCC strategy ► Definition of a strategy planning process

Table 9.1 CCC Vision and CCC Strategy Development Service

9.2.2 CCC Assessment

This customer-specific SAP service forms the basis for a customized implementation of your CCC vision and strategy. For this reason, you first must get an overview and status of the business processes, IT landscape, IT services, strategies, and structures of your enterprise. You then determine the improvement recommendations that arise from your enterprise situation for the existing or planned SAP CCC. The results are used as the starting point for the *CCC Setup and Development Service* (see the following section).

Challenges	Benefits	Results
► Comparison of own CCC performance and comparison group ► Determination of the improvement potentials	► Joint analysis of the CCC degree of maturity ► Access to industry best practices	► Determination of the CCC degree of maturity ► Identified and evaluated improvement measures in examined fields of activity

Table 9.2 CCC Assessment Service

9.2.3　CCC Setup and CCC Development

This service provides you with a customized support for the setup and reorganization of SAP CCC. The CCC strategy and individual requirements of your enterprise are implemented consistently. Best practices and structured procedures ensure that your service and support organization will provide a sustained value contribution.

Challenges	Benefits	Results
▶ Improvement of the SAP operation's effectiveness and efficiency ▶ Preparation of the CCC organization for the CCC recertification	▶ Joint implementation of improvement potentials	▶ Improvement of identified fields of activity

Table 9.3　CCC Setup and CCC Development Service

9.2.4　Solution Operations Readiness Assessment (SORA)

This standardized service checks whether all essential conditions have been met for a successful go-live within an SAP implementation project; it particularly analyzes the processes of IT service and application management as well as the tools used. The results are recorded in an action plan.

Challenge	Benefits	Results
Identification of fields of activity during SAP implementation projects prior to going live	▶ Optimization of handover planning ▶ Recommendations and best practices for operation	▶ Suggestions for optimizing the handover planning ▶ Identified and evaluated improvement measures in predefined fields of activity

Table 9.4　Operations Readiness Assessment Service

9.2.5　Solution Operations Competence Assessment (SOCA)

This standardized service analyzes the efficiency of the existing CCC organization, in particular for the processes of IT service and application management as well as the tools used.

Here as well, the results are recorded in an action plan.

Challenge	Benefits	Results
Identification of fields of activity for the SAP operation	► Increase in efficiency of the SAP operation ► Recommendations and best practices for operation	► Suggestions for optimizing the SAP operation ► Identified and evaluated improvement measures in predefined fields of activity

Table 9.5 Operations Competence Assessment Service

9.2.6 CCC Certification

The CCC certification service conducted by SAP confirms that the performance levels of the competence center have been reached. During an audit, all relevant CCC functions are checked and evaluated. You are presented with a certification document after successful completion.

Challenge	Benefits	Results
Achieving the criteria for certification of the CCC organization	Use of the CCC program benefits (see Section 8.3)	CCC certificate

Table 9.6 CCC Certification Service

9.2.7 CCC E2E Operations Certification

This certification service checks the required end-to-end abilities of the employees and the degree of maturity of the basic IT service and application management processes by means of a Solution Operations Competence Assessment (SOCA).

Challenge	Benefits	Results
Differentiated identification of concrete strengths and weaknesses of the support organization	Identification of improvement potential, development of an action plan	► CCC E2E operations certificate ► Suggestions for optimizing the SAP operation ► Identified and evaluated improvement measures in predefined fields of activity

Table 9.7 CCC E2E Operations Certification Service

9.3 CCC Certification Program

The obligation to set up SAP CCC is stipulated in a contract between SAP and a customer. SAP conducts a certification as proof of the successful installation.

SAP offers a two-level certification for this purpose. Until recently, the certification only checked whether general support functions, such as Service Desk, contract processing, internal marketing, and development coordination, had been established successfully. A second certification level, which has been available since 2007, checks the detailed strengths and weaknesses of a support organization.

Figure 9.2 illustrates a possible action plan to achieve the higher certification level.

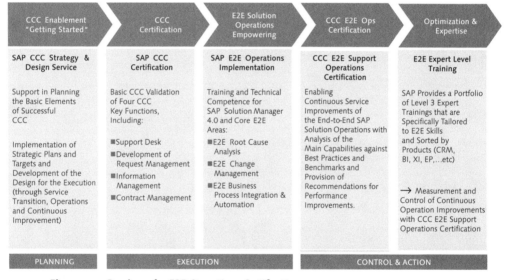

Figure 9.2 Roadmap for E2E Operations Certification

For certification, a distinction is made between *initial certification* and *recertification*.

▶ **Initial Certification**
The initial certification is carried out in the form of an audit. This audit follows the currently valid certification criteria and includes the following:

▸ Interviews and verification of the answers to the questions on the checklist. The checklist includes question with regard to SAP CCC and must be completed by the customer in advance. The answers are checked by SAP together with the respective contacts using the appropriate systems.

▸ Check whether the required score has been reached.

Currently, the following basic functions are certified:

▸ Information management

▸ Contract management

▸ Coordination of development requests

▸ Support Desk

The certification is valid for two years. A recertification is required when this period has expired.

▸ **Recertification**
The SAP CCC certification is a recurring activity. A recertification is required when a maximum of two years has expired. The recertification can be conducted on-site or remote. For this purpose, the SAP CCC must complete the current checklist and send it to the responsible CCC certification auditor. During the remote audit, the auditor checks and verifies the answers to the questions on the checklist as well as the compliance with the support desk criteria.

If the recertification is conducted remotely, the SAP certification service is free of charge, provided an effort of one person day isn't exceeded.

9.3.1 CCC E2E Operations Certification

Whereas the standard CCC certification checks mandatory abilities of the CCC organization, the *CCC-E2E-Operations certification* analyzes the implemented SAP solution competence in detail. The extended certification enables you to identify strengths and weaknesses, to compare the existing abilities with benchmarks and best practices, and to draw up plans for optimizing the end-to-end solution competence in cooperation with SAP experts.

During this certification, SAP checks the qualifications of the employees and the degree of maturity of the established processes directly at the customer's site. The customer must provide certificates to prove the qualification of the employees.

9.3.2 Benefits of Certified SAP CCCs

Certified SAP CCCs provide numerous benefits, for example:

- Reduced maintenance fees
- Integration with the development of the SAP service portfolio
- Participation in ramp-up validation tests
- Intensive knowledge transfer about relevant topics, for example, WebEx sessions
- Access to best practices and customer satisfaction reports
- Access to online knowledge products, even if the customer does not implement a ramp-up project
- Prioritized treatment of messages in the processing procedure

This list is continuously enhanced and published in CCCNet at *http://service.sap.com/CCCNet*.

9.4 Summary

You are provided with numerous services for establishing your SAP CCC. An extensive community is available for exchanging knowledge, for example, America's SAP User Group (ASUG). Moreover, SAP directly offers a service portfolio that supports you in all phases (planning, building, running) of the CCC setup. Ultimately, you can obtain an SAP certification that documents the quality of your CCC processes and includes benefits for reduced maintenance fees.

10 Outlook

Innovation is the differentiation factor in current and future competition. Business models must respond quickly to new and changing market requirements to implement innovation and to master the three central requirements: deregulation, globalization, and commoditization. Only then can you ensure the competitiveness of your enterprise in the long term. IT is important because it must support the innovation of the enterprise through flexible, integrative IT architectures and contribute to the overall productivity increase of the enterprise through the industrialization of customer-specific processes.

SAP's response to flexible IT architectures is enterprise service-oriented architecture (enterprise SOA). The concept of enterprise SOA is based on the modularization of software components in services that are provided to the different systems and applications and can be dynamically combined to form new business processes.

The implementation of enterprise SOA requires changes to the IT. In addition to the creation of necessary infrastructures, you must structure the new tasks and map them in roles. Figure 10.1 shows the development of roles based on a layer model. These roles are described in greater detail in Appendix A.

To create scope for IT innovations you must identify potentials for reducing costs and implement them sustainably. Essential factors in this context are the standardization and consolidation at all levels as well as the selective outsourcing of processes that are not in the primary focus.

This trend is not new; by contrast, the increased necessity for consolidation is new because growing complex IT landscapes are no longer manageable as would be required for supporting key business processes.

At the same time, manufacturers of hardware, software, and tools for supporting the IT service management processes have recognized the necessity for consolidation and offer corresponding products and services. Examples are the virtualization of servers; the integration options via interfaces, for example, SAP NetWeaver Exchange Infrastructure (SAP NetWeaver XI); the support of routine tasks in the application operation by means of SAP Solution Manager, and the definition and setup of process standards with *SAP Standards for Solution Operations*.

Layers	Description	Today – Roles with Business Skills +IT	Today – Roles with IT Skills +Business	Future (Enterprise SOA) – Roles with Business Skills +IT	Future (Enterprise SOA) – Roles with IT Skills +Business
Domain	■ Management of the Domains as Logically Linked Units within IT and Business			■ Business Domain Owner	■ Domain IT Responsible
Business Processes	■ Strategic Management of the Business Process Landscape to Support the Future Business Models ■ Detailed Business Process Management for an Optimum Interaction with the Enterprise Services	■ Business Process Analyst ■ Business Process Architect ■ Business Process Owner		■ Business Process Analyst ■ Business Process Architect ■ Business Process Owner	
Enterprise Services	■ Management and Maintenance of the Entire Enterprise Service Portfolio ■ Management and Maintenance of the Enterprise Services for Continuous Support of Business Processes				■ Enterprise Service Portfolio Manager ■ Enterprise Service Owner (Provider)
Service Architecture	■ Architecture Management for the Enterprise Service Platform (Service, Data, Application, ... Architecture)				■ Enterprise Service Architect
Applications	■ Development of Enterprise Services ■ Testing and Quality Assurance		■ Enterprise Service Developer ■ Enterprise Service Tester		■ Enterprise Service Developer ■ Enterprise Service Tester
Infrastructure	■ Management and Provision of the IT Infrastructure		■ IT Infrastructure Architect		■ IT Infrastructure Architect

Figure 10.1 Enterprise SOA Role Model

However, the services must be adapted, too, for example, the establishing *SAP Expertise on Demand*. More than 40% of the queries to SAP support do not concern problems. The customers rather request short-term consultation with the SAP experts on topics such as business process design, performance optimization, installation services, and so on. Using SAP Expertise on Demand enables the customer to revert to the entire SAP network via SAP Solution Manager and to integrate this network in the customer-specific processes as a back office.

Figure 10.2 shows that the entire customer organization can benefit from this service. For example, SAP Value Engineering Services can be used in the Program Management Office to identify the potentials of using SAP solutions.

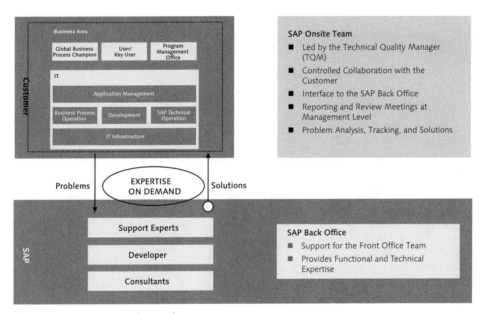

Figure 10.2 Expertise on Demand

The demand for supporting innovation capacity and flexibility and the integration and productivity increases change the entire IT. In this context, SAP CCC, which constitutes a link between business areas and IT, becomes an essential driving force. This necessitates the further development of tasks and the organization of SAP CCC — a *next generation CCC*.

Appendices

A Roles

This appendix describes the different roles of SAP CCC, subdivided according to business area, IT, and enterprise SOA.

A.1 Business Area: User

A.1.1 Task

The term *user* describes the user of a business solution. It includes all roles within an enterprise and, where appropriate, partners of the enterprise authorized to use the solution, for example, customers or vendors. Users are generally those persons who make use of the services of the support organization on a daily basis.

A.1.2 Basic Responsibilities and Activities

▸ The user must have a sound training to be able to use the SAP solution in daily business operation.

▸ The user must know how to treat problem situations and unpredictable emergencies (e.g., how he can contact the key user or Service Desk).

A.2 Business Area: Key User

A.2.1 Task

The *key user* is an expert in the deployment of an application and usually belongs to a business area. In comparison to his peers, the key user has more experience and knowledge about the application ("primus inter pares," first among equals). The key user is responsible for supporting users in the effective use of business processes. He is the first contact point if problems or questions arise.

A.2.2 Basic Responsibilities and Activities

▸ Answers to practical user questions

▸ Primary contact for the communication of problems to the support organization

- Individual treatment of incidents in case of escalation (individual incident escalation)
- Maintains master data
- Responsible for interfaces to other applications in the running business operation
- Tests new versions, functions, and amendments prior to use in production
- Transfers knowledge about new or modified functions to users
- Provides input for the definition and modification of business processes
- Communicates any kind of configuration requirement

A.2.3 Skills

- Full comprehension of the processes of the corresponding work area
- Sound knowledge about process flow and the options of user-specific settings in the SAP solution
- Sound knowledge about the key support processes, particularly those concerning managing problems, reporting incidents, and handling incidents

Key users typically participate in an implementation project (process workshop, user acceptance tests, etc.) where they gain extensive knowledge about the business solution. After they return to their usual role, they can support other users when problems or questions arise.

A.3 Business Area: Business Process Champion (Business Domain Owner, Business Process Expert)

A.3.1 Task

The *business process champion* is a member of the business area that can typically be found at the management level. He is responsible for the content of a process and for the business activity that is mapped by means of the process. Moreover, he is responsible for ensuring that all employees of the business area have a high degree of knowledge. This is indispensable to avoid problems and to ensure the smooth flow of processes.

A.3.2 Basic Responsibilities and Activities

▸ Defines specific business processes

▸ Evaluates and approves changes to specific business processes

▸ Ensures that problems and requirements with regard to the processes are prioritized and communicated to the support organization.

▸ Maintains effective communication channels between the business area and the support organization

▸ Monitors the performance and effectiveness of specific business processes in close cooperation with the support organization

▸ Triggers and manages escalations

▸ Provides regular user assessments and proper training

A.3.3 Skills

▸ Profound comprehension for the specific business processes

▸ Extensive knowledge of the system's process flow

▸ Extensive knowledge about the system processes triggered by the business processes and how they are prioritized in the system

▸ Understands full overview of the structures of the support organization and of the key support processes

▸ Detailed knowledge about the procedure in case of escalations and knowledge about the escalation criteria

▸ Excellent communication and contact skills

A.4 IT: Service Desk Agent

A.4.1 Task

The *service desk agent* is a member of the Service Desk and represents the business area's starting point for communication with the support organization. Communication for all topics that require the attention of the support organization starts here.

A.4.2 Basic Responsibilities and Activities

All stages of the incident lifecycle:

- Records incidents
- Logs incidents
- Makes initial estimates of incidents
- Searches for a solution in the internal database
- Searches for SAP Notes
- Provides a solution or forwarding
- Tracks progress
- Completes incidents
- Continuously notifies the customer during the process

A.4.3 Skills

- Very good communication and contact skills, particularly for direct contact with the customer
- Full knowledge of the local and country-specific requirements and the ability to explain them to the support organization that processes the incident, if required
- High degree of adaptability
- Ability to maintain good relationships with the business area and to understand the effects on the business
- Ability to provide all relevant information to the responsible contacts in the support organization
- Profound IT skills and first-level knowledge about the products and applications of the customers
- Knowledge of business terminology that is used in the enterprise
- Readiness for continuous further training and to keep up-to-date about the developments of products and programs
- Second language, if this is required for the enterprise's business
- Skills for the use of internal communication means (e.g., email)

A.5 IT: Application Management Expert

A.5.1 Task

The *application management expert* is a member of the support team. He has expert knowledge of certain applications and uses it to support daily business operation and the effective performance of the business solution.

A.5.2 Basic Responsibilities and Activities

▶ **Operational support activities**

  ▶ Coordinates and implements application tests in close cooperation with the technology team

  ▶ Evaluates, tests, implements, and verifies change requests

  ▶ Maintains suitable documentation

  ▶ Verifies and implements recommendations in service reports in cooperation with the technology team

  ▶ Provides second-level support for applications

A.5.3 Skills

▶ Detailed functional knowledge of the management and monitoring of applications

▶ Detailed knowledge of application tests, test procedures, and test scenarios (new support packages, releases, functions, and adaptations)

▶ Detailed knowledge of internal support processes and escalation processes

▶ Knowledge of SAP support processes and escalation processes

▶ Knowledge of projects or experience in project management

▶ Knowledge of the definition and rollout of standards and templates

▶ Knowledge and competence for the use of SAP Solution Manager

▶ Conversance with the change management of business processes, including implementing, testing, and verifying change requests

A.6   IT: Business Process Expert

A.6.1   Task

The *business process expert (IT)* is a member of the support team. He has expert knowledge of certain processes and uses it to support daily business operation and the effective performance of the business solution.

A.6.2   Basic Responsibilities and Activities

► **Operational support activities**

  ► Designs, specifies, tests, and implements changes to the business processes

  ► Maintains suitable documentation

  ► Verifies and implements recommendations in service reports in cooperation with the technology team

  ► Monitors, analyzes, tunes, and optimizes business processes and interfaces in close cooperation with the technology team

► **Project-supporting activities**

  ► Designs and implements business processes

  ► Defines and rolls out standards and templates

A.6.3   Skills

► Detailed functional knowledge of the management and monitoring of business processes

► Detailed knowledge of internal support processes and escalation processes

► Knowledge of SAP support processes and escalation processes

► Knowledge of projects or experience in project management

► Knowledge of design and implementation of business processes

► Knowledge of the definition and rollout of standards and templates

► Knowledge and competence for the use of SAP Solution Manager

A.7 IT: Interface/Integration Expert

A.7.1 Task

The *interface/integration expert* is responsible for the implementation and operational management of interfaces within the business solution. This typically includes the coordination of activities relating to technology and application. The interface/integration expert provides expertise for the support of daily business and for ensuring the effective performance of interfaces.

A.7.2 Basic Responsibilities and Activities

▶ Defines and implements the business process interfaces

▶ Defines, implements, and monitors the application management processes

▶ Maintains the required entries of interfaces in SAP Solution Manager

▶ Provides second-level support for interfaces

A.7.3 Skills

▶ Detailed knowledge of interface technologies

▶ Detailed knowledge of the definition, implementation, and operation of business process interfaces

▶ Detailed knowledge of the analysis and optimization of business process interfaces

▶ Detailed knowledge of internal support processes and escalation processes

▶ Knowledge of SAP support processes and escalation processes

▶ Knowledge of the management and monitoring of business processes/applications

▶ Knowledge of application tests, test procedures, and test scenarios (new support packages, releases, functions, and adaptations)

▶ Knowledge of projects or experience in project management

▶ Knowledge of design and implementation of business processes

▶ Knowledge of the definition and rollout of standards and templates

▶ Knowledge and competence for the use of SAP Solution Manager

▶ Conversance with the change management of business processes, including implementing, testng, and verifying change requests

A.8 IT: Technology Expert

A.8.1 Task

A *technology expert* is responsible for the design, planning, setup, and technical support of SAP-centered solutions and their interfaces. He acts based on the technical and business requirements.

A.8.2 Basic Responsibilities and Activities

▶ Designs, plans, and implements the technical infrastructure

▶ Makes technical adaptation to SAP solutions

▶ Defines, plans, and implements system operations

A.8.3 Skills

▶ Detailed knowledge of the technical infrastructure and interfaces

▶ Detailed knowledge of system operations

▶ Detailed knowledge of performance management

▶ Detailed knowledge of change management

▶ Knowledge of internal support processes and escalation processes

▶ Knowledge of SAP support processes and escalation processes

A.9 IT: Technical Administrator

A.9.1 Task

The *technical administrator* is responsible for the administration and operation of the SAP-centered solution. In addition, he participates in implementation projects to support the technology expert and to ensure a smooth transfer from the implementation to production operation.

A.9.2 Basic Responsibilities and Activities

▶ Sets up the technical infrastructure

▶ Installs and configures software and hardware

▶ Plans hardware capacity

▶ Implements and tests backup and recovery concepts, high availability solutions, as well as network, database, and operating system configurations

▶ Organizes SAP Basis, middleware, and output devices (printers, fax, etc.)

▶ Makes technical adaptations to SAP solutions

▶ Makes technical adaptations of interfaces and support

▶ Maintains technical system information in service tools (e.g., SAPNet-R/3 frontend)

▶ Performs operation and administration functions

▶ Performs system, performance, and change management functions

▶ Verifies and implements recommendations in service reports

▶ Provides technical second-level support

▶ Provides remote access for SAP

A.9.3 Skills

▶ Knowledge of the technical infrastructure

▶ Knowledge of the installation and configuration of software and hardware

▶ Knowledge of the hardware capacity planning

▶ Knowledge of backup and recovery

▶ Knowledge of high availability solutions

▶ Knowledge of network, database, and operating system configuration

▶ Knowledge of SAP Basis, middleware, and output devices (printers, fax, etc.)

▶ Detailed knowledge of the operation and administration of solutions

▶ Detailed knowledge of system management

▶ Detailed knowledge of performance management

▶ Knowledge of change management

▶ Knowledge of internal support processes and escalation processes

▶ Knowledge of SAP support processes and escalation processes

A.10 IT: Development Expert

A.10.1 Task

The main task of the *development expert* is to develop improvements, modifications, user exits, and reports to the customer's requirements. Moreover, he supports the incident resolution process.

A.10.2 Basic Responsibilities and Activities

▶ Develops customer-specific improvements, changes, user exits, and reports

▶ Provides technical implementation of SAPNet Notes

▶ Provides expert knowledge in case of problems that are caused by nonstandard code

▶ Corrects problems that are caused by nonstandard code

▶ Supports upgrades with regard to modifications

▶ Configures interfaces

A.10.3 Skills

Depending on the activities to be implemented:

▶ **Overview of basic technologies**

    ▶ ABAP Workbench and Dictionary

    ▶ Processes in development projects

    ▶ Technologies of list processing

    ▶ Dialog programming

    ▶ Database dialogs (for reading and changing the database)

    ▶ Improvements and modifications

    ▶ Interfaces for data transfer

- **Advanced programming**
  - Technologies of list processing
  - Dialog programming
  - Database changes
  - Improvements and modifications
- **Overview of SAP interface development**
  - Remote Function Calls (RFC)
  - Application Link Enabling (ALE)
  - Business Connector
- **SAP models of Web programming**
  - Internet Transaction Server sRFC
  - Web Application Server
  - Portals
  - Analysis and optimization of Web applications
  - Review and certification tests
- **Implementation of workflows and general overview**
  - SAP Business Workflow Architecture
  - Workflow implementation projects using ASAP
  - Business Workplace
  - Workflow design
  - Workflow templates, wizards, and ad-hoc functions
  - Development environment and Business Object Repository
  - Single-level or multi-level activities, events, containers, and routing
  - Organization management and roles
  - System runtime
  - Reporting and workflow information system
  - Configuration, administration, tuning, and troubleshooting
  - Integration technologies for SAP Business Workflows

A.11 Enterprise SOA: Enterprise Service Developer

A.11.1 Task

The *enterprise service developer* develops and maintains services in compliance with the enterprise SOA lifecycle. Moreover, he implements the services according to the implementation and enterprise SOA guidelines and provides technical skills related to the products.

A.11.2 Basic Responsibilities and Activities

▶ Converts business processes to operational service designs

▶ Creates and tests services/evaluation of performance tests

▶ Cooperates with the enterprise architects to improve the design

▶ Creates all necessary integration logics to assign them to the underlying application services

▶ Implements services

▶ Uses the integration platform tools, for example, SAP NetWeaver

▶ Develops prototypes

A.11.3 Skills

▶ **Specialist skills**

  ▷ Conversion of designs to developments

  ▷ Knowledge of enterprise SOA structures, repositories, designs, and interfaces

  ▷ Experience with SAP NetWeaver portal design

  ▷ Development skills (e.g., HTML, HTMLB, ABAP-OO, BPEL, BSP, JAVA, SOAP-XML, UI, UML, WSDL)

  ▷ Design and development of Web user interfaces (Web Dynpro)

  ▷ Implementation of Web Services

  ▷ Understanding of process integration, for example, SAP NetWeaver Process Integration (SAP NetWeaver PI)

  ▷ Knowledge of BAPIs, PROXIES, and ARIS modeling

- **Methodological skills**
  - Project support: implementation and testing
- **Soft skills**
  - Time management, task planning, and prioritization
  - Cross-functional thinking
  - Ability to work in a team, communication, and cooperation

A.12 Enterprise SOA: Enterprise Service Tester

A.12.1 Task

The main task of the *enterprise service tester* is to certify services with regard to their conformity to business requirements.

A.12.2 Basic Responsibilities and Activities

- Safeguards the proper functioning of services
- Ensures the appropriate Quality of Service (QoS)
- Manages complex and shared test environments
- Works with the SAP Test Workbench for any type of test, for example, regression test, integration test
- Controls performance and regression tests
- Ensures the quality of services and the service documentation, including the service lifecycle

A.12.3 Skills

- **Specialist skills**
  - Knowledge of enterprise SOA structures, repositories, business processes
  - Understanding of process integration
  - Knowledge of ARIS modeling
- **Methodological skills**
  - Knowledge of quality management
  - Project support: implementation and test

▶ **Soft skills**

  ▸ Cross-functional thinking

  ▸ Ability to work in a team, communication, and cooperation

A.13 Enterprise SOA: IT Infrastructure Architect (Technical Architect)

A.13.1 Task

An *IT infrastructure architect* provides the technical basis, that is, the basic infrastructure, to implement business processes, control information, and operate company systems. In addition, he maintains the architectural consistency of enterprise services.

A.13.2 Basic Responsibilities and Activities

▶ Develops and maintains the vision for enterprise SOA and the enterprise SOA platform

▶ Develops plans to achieve the future enterprise SOA platform based on today's application platform

▶ Further trains for new enterprise SOA products and technologies and cooperates with enterprise service developers to define what is to be integrated with the enterprise SOA platform

▶ Comprehends and solves all technical infrastructure and architecture problems for services

▶ Defines infrastructure services to support the implementation of business services

▶ Defines implementation patterns for all supported application environments

A.13.3 Skills

▶ **Specialist skills**

  ▸ Knowledge of architecture principles of services within the enterprise SOA concept

- ▸ Knowledge of service lifecycles, service design, implementation standards, and security concepts
- ▸ **Methodological skills**
  - ▸ Profitability and user-oriented problem analysis and solution
- ▸ **Soft skills**
  - ▸ Cross-functional thinking
  - ▸ Ability to work in a team, communication, and cooperation

A.14 Enterprise SOA: Enterprise Service Portfolio Manager

A.14.1 Task

The *enterprise service portfolio manager* develops and maintains the entire service portfolio. He uses standards and promotes the development of new services according to customer requirements. Additionally, he ensures an enterprisewide understanding of the available and future services.

A.14.2 Basic Responsibilities and Activities

- ▸ Controls the selection of new services and sorts existing services
- ▸ Uses numerous portfolio management criteria, such as flexibility, number of services, and so on, to ensure the value and quality of enterprise services
- ▸ Controls use-of-potential analysis of enterprise services
- ▸ Checks whether existing services meet the necessary business requirements
- ▸ Implements analyses with regard to enterprise service requirements
- ▸ Identifies and uses market opportunities; identifies portfolio gaps
- ▸ Manages global service portfolio process and framework

A.14.3 Skills

- ▸ **Specialist skills**
  - ▸ Knowledge of business processes
  - ▸ Knowledge of ARIS modeling
  - ▸ Controlling

- **Methodological skills**
  - Process analysis, modeling, and optimization
  - Implementation of prioritizations
  - Business case calculation and control
  - Profitability and user-oriented problem analysis and solution
  - Methodological procedure (methodological approaches, structures, self-management, etc.)
- **Soft skills**
  - Logical thinking
  - Moderation
  - Presentation
  - Interview

A.15   Enterprise SOA: Enterprise Service Owner

A.15.1   Task

The task of the *enterprise service owner* includes the provision of enterprise services for business process owners and for the party that orders the services. Furthermore, he is responsible for the continuous improvement of the service development and provision.

A.15.2   Basic Responsibilities and Activities

- Serves as counterpart to the business process owner
- Controls the identification, development, use, maintenance, and support of enterprise services to meet the requirements of the business areas
- Defines and monitors service level agreements (SLAs) for enterprise services
- Cooperates with the business areas to identify the most essential business events that are supported by enterprise services
- Determines the correct use of services that are required for certain business scenarios
- Provides and develops enterprise services

A.15.3 Skills

▶ **Specialist skills**

 ▶ Potentials and functional principles of enterprise applications

 ▶ IT knowledge of enterprise SOA structures, concepts, structures, and repositories

 ▶ Experience with portal design and development

 ▶ Interface know-how

 ▶ Experience with enterprise SOA system architectures

 ▶ Understanding of process integration, for example, SAP NetWeaver PI

 ▶ Knowledge of ARIS modeling

▶ **Methodological skills**

 ▶ Project support: design phase

▶ **Soft skills**

 ▶ Time management, task planning, prioritization

 ▶ Service orientation

 ▶ Cross-functional thinking

 ▶ Ability to work in a team, communication, and cooperation

A.16   Enterprise SOA: Enterprise Service Architect

A.16.1 Task

The *enterprise service architect* transforms the enterprise from a classical IT enterprise to an enterprise SOA business. In doing so, he ensures a continuous reconciliation of business areas and IT and identifies essential driving factors.

A.16.2 Basic Responsibilities and Activities

▶ Ensures a commitment to enterprise SOA and convinces others of this commitment

▶ Defines the framework for the success of enterprise SOA

▶ Promotes the enterprise SOA process

▶ Analyzes the existing IT architecture, market trends, and new technologies

▶ Defines and develops the IT strategy in close cooperation with decision makers

▶ Understands, defends, and supports the IT strategy

▶ Provides the business operation basis to achieve continuous business process innovation

▶ Defines governance

A.16.3 Skills

▶ **Specialist skills**

  ▶ Understanding of business processes and their implications on the architecture

  ▶ Ability to transform business requirements to architecture requirements

  ▶ Information management

  ▶ Communication to promote the enterprise SOA process

  ▶ Promotion of the use of enterprise SOA and ensuring compliance with the defined architecture

  ▶ Profound IT understanding

  ▶ Enterprise SOA frameworks (e.g., TOGAF)

▶ **Methodological skills**

  ▶ Ability to provide results: short-, medium-, and long-term

  ▶ Strong leadership qualities

  ▶ Ability to keep the balance of the "big picture" and short-term activities

▶ **Soft skills**

  ▶ Time management, task planning, prioritization

  ▶ Conflict and crisis management

  ▶ Innovative and cross-functional thinking

B Management of Global SAP Templates

Section 5.7 in Chapter 5 described the targets and tasks of the change management process. In this context, the issue of the request process structure and change management within SAP template projects always arises.

To support the global expansion, create new flexibility and enterprise wide reporting structures, and reduce the complexity of the SAP landscape, a lot of globally active enterprises choose to create a global SAP template.

B.1 Concepts and Scenarios

To begin our discussion, the following list briefly describes the necessary concepts and design scenarios:

▶ **SAP system**
An SAP system comprises an installed SAP solution, for example, SAP ERP or SAP Customer Relationship Management (SAP CRM), that is characterized by an independent database and a set of processes.

▶ **SAP client**
In commercial, organizational, and technical terms, an SAP client is a self-contained unit in an SAP system with a shared set of tables and separate master records for each independent unit.

▶ **SAP template**
An SAP template is a template for an SAP system or an SAP client with predefined repository objects (such as programs, structures) and Customizing settings. Local or industry-specific requirements are integrated with the derived systems on the basis of SAP templates. This applies particularly to application tables, Customizing, profiles, authorizations, and reporting variants.

Figure B.1 shows three possible alternatives to map technical requirements in SAP landscapes.

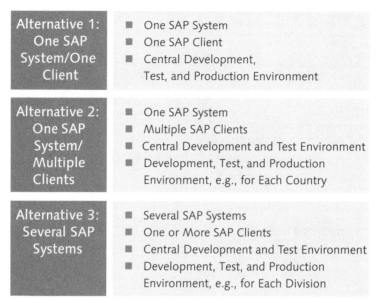

Figure B.1 Alternatives for Mapping Technical Requirements

Customers, in particular, with comparable products, similar customer structures, and uniform business processes, map their business processes in one SAP system with only one SAP client (alternative 1).

If multiple SAP clients are mapped on one SAP system (alterative 2), you can support different customer and product structures in similar business processes and uniform data standards, for example.

Mapping of SAP clients in several SAP systems (alternative 3) supports comprehensive independence of decentralized units. Examples for such units include different regions, divisions, or production locations.

Against the background of the alternatives mentioned, there are two useful options to describe an SAP template: *on the basis of an SAP system or on the basis of an SAP client.*

No matter whether you describe it on the basis of an SAP system or an SAP client, the implementation of an SAP template always provides numerous technical and IT benefits, for example:

▶ The business process variants are reduced.

▶ Innovative business processes can be implemented much faster.

- The prerequisites for shared services structures are better.
- IT operating costs are reduced.
- Test activities are reduced.
- The maintainability of the SAP landscape improves.

To use these benefits, you must implement the following critical success factors:

- Identify and communicate the requirement to standardize and harmonize.
- Continuously support the initiative via the global and local management team, in user departments and IT.
- Create a global team under the management of the user departments to develop a global design.
- Process harmonization and standardization before the start of the project.
- Provide early design of uniform roles, trainings, security profiles, and functional requirements.
- Provide optimum support of local characteristics.
- Reduce the release frequency to one to two releases per year.
- Support the activities via professional organizational change management.

The definition and the rollout of an SAP template already represent a major challenge. In addition, the long-term operation requires new, extended governance structures, particularly for the coordination of technical requirements and changes. For this purpose, you need to create effective and efficient structures and procedures that meet central as well as country- or division-specific requirements. Decision and escalation roles and processes need to be transparent here.

The following sections use a customer example to illustrate how you can design a change process for an SAP template. In this context, the release process of SAP template requests is particularly analyzed. An SAP template request is considered a request that results in a change or extension of a global SAP template.

The schematic sample system environment is shown in Figure B.2. This environment is characterized by a global development and test environment for the SAP template as well as by a three-system landscape that consists of a development, test, and production environment for each division.

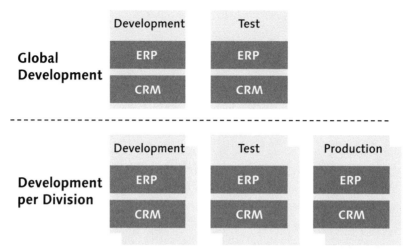

Figure B.2 Sample System Environment

In the example provided, an organizational unit similar to the program management office shown in Figure 4.2 of Chapter 4 has been created that centrally defines the processes and procedures that are necessary for the operation of the SAP template, such as the request process, and is operationally responsible for them.

B.2   Request Process

The request process is the initial step within the change management process. Requests go through the following high-level process:

1. Key users create the request.
2. The business process champion releases the request locally.
3. The program management office valuates the request and provides a global recommendation.
4. The change advisory board releases the request globally.

That means that key users first create a request supported by a workflow. Among other things, this request contains information on incident, problem, or change references; the process level of the effects of the request; and an initial categorization and prioritization.

You distinguish between the following change categories:

▶ **Standard service**

Standard services are performed by the Program Management Office and other organizational units. They include, for example, the central user administration, the setup of printer connections, a central translation service, and training for the users. A list of these services is stored in a service catalog.

▶ **Standard change**

There is a detailed and approved procedure instruction for every standard change. The risks can be neglected, and the costs are known.

▶ **Other changes**

Other changes are planned changes that aren't standard services or standard changes.

The request involves an initial categorization into the following classes:

▶ **Operational changes**

Request of the category of continuous operational changes particularly comprise standard services and standard changes. This classification also decides whether a request needs to be released locally or centrally via the Program Management Office and the change advisory board.

▶ **Changes within a release or rollout project**

Changes within release or rollout projects are bundled by the Program Management Office and implemented by means of release planning based on a release calendar.

To prioritize the request, the requesting unit uses the priority matrix shown in Figure B.3.

Category \ Priority	High	Medium	Low
Legal Requirements	Legal Requirements (Implementation within 3 Months)	Legal Requirements (Implementation within 6 Months)	Legal Requirements (Implementation within 12 Months)
Necessary Requirements	Interface to a Local System, Prerequisite for Rollout Project	Reporting Requirement, Process Optimization	New Process Functionality
Useful Requirements	Return on Investment (ROI) < 3 Years	Qualitative Benefit, Positive Net Present Value	Qualitative Benefit, Negative Net Present Value

Figure B.3 Priority Matrix

The Program Management Office distinguishes two main request categories:

▶ Continuous operational changes

▶ Changes within releases or rollout projects

After the process champion has released the request, the Program Management Office valuates the request. Then, it creates a cost/benefit analysis on the basis of a coordinated structure.

This matrix lays the foundation for releasing requests to further develop the SAP template. For requests with a volume of more than $100,000, a business case is created.

A detailed request process ensures a high level of flexibility of the local business areas.

C   Literature

Achim Töpfer, *Six Sigma* (Springer 2007).

Active Global Support, *Standardized E2E Solution Operations* (Marketplace, 2007).

ASUG/SAP, *Centers of Excellence (CoE) Outsourcing Survey* (2007).

ASUG/SAP, *Centers of Excellence (CoE) Benchmarking and Best Practices* (2006).

Boris Otto, Sven Winkler, Jörg Wolter, *Succeeding with your SAP NetWeaver Portal Project - Best Practices for Design, Composition, and Operation* (SAP PRESS, 2006).

Diane Morello, *The IT Professional Outlook* (Gartner Research, 2005).

Gerhard Oswald, *SAP Service and Support*, 3rd ed. (SAP PRESS, 2006).

Isabell Jäger, Rolf Schumann, Werner Tiki Küstenmacher, *Simplify your IT* (Campus 2006).

Liane Will, Sigrid Hagemann, *SAP R/3 System Administration*, 2nd ed. (SAP PRESS, 2003).

Marc O. Schäfer, Matthias Melich, *SAP Solution Manager* (SAP PRESS, 2006).

Martin Kütz, Andreas Meier, *IT-Controlling* (dpunkt, 2007).

Richard Nolan, Warren McFarlan, *Building an IT Governance Committee* (Harvard Business Review, 2005).

Rolf-Dieter Kempis, Jürgen Ringbeck, *Do IT Smart* (Ueberreuter 1998).

Sabine Schöler, Liane Will, *SAP IT Service & Application Management* (SAP PRESS, 2005).

Sabine Schöler, Liane Will, Marc O. Schäfer, *CobiT and the Sarbanes-Oxley Act* (SAP PRESS 2007).

SAP, *CCC Manual, http://service.sap.com/cccnet (2007).*

Vital Anderhub, *Service Level Management* (SAP PRESS, 2006).

D   The Authors

 **Boris Otto** is a project manager at the Institute of Information Management at the University of St. Gallen, Switzerland. His major areas of research comprise business engineering and corporate IT management. Prior to this position, he worked as a Principal Business Consultant at SAP Business Consulting focusing on IT strategy and program management assignments for large enterprises. Moreover, he was head of the Competence Center Electronic Business Integration at the Fraunhofer Institute for Industrial Engineering and worked as a Consultant at PricewaterhouseCoopers.

 **Jörg Wolter** works for INFO AG, an SAP Partner company, heading the innovation and service development group. His work focuses on IT service portfolio, IT innovations, IT service management, and program management for SAP implementations. Before that, he was a Principal Business Consultant at SAP Business Consulting. His responsibilities included the development of the SAP CCC service portfolio, and he was involved in a range of SAP Customer Competence Center implementations for large enterprises. He is certified ITIL service manager and Six Sigma black belt.

Index

Provides managers and consultants with a complete guide to what SAP CRM is

Teaches about the benefits of using CRM to build profitable customer relationships

Includes practical insights from customers using SAP CRM successfully

Srini Katta

Discover SAP CRM

The book provides manager, consultants, power users, and aspiring users with a detailed guide to all things CRM, including what it is, why SAP CRM is important, and what the many application interfaces are (Call Center, E-Commerce, Mobile, and Channel). The book teaches about the core areas of CRM, including marketing, sales, and service, and explains the different ways SAP CRM can be used and integrated into a business. It also explains the technology and tools behind CRM (Netweaver, Web Services, Business Server Pages, Java, ABAP, etc.), and covers the various user access modes used to utilize the applications (desktop, laptop, tablet PC, PDA, & smartphone).

406 pp., 2008, 39,95 Euro / US$ 39.95
ISBN 978-1-59229-173-1

>> www.sap-press.de/1641

Provides a complete guide for optimizing and customizing your SAP CRM Interaction Center

Answers all of your Frequently-Asked-Questions

Includes real-world examples and success stories

John Burton, John Burton

Maximizing Your SAP CRM Interaction Center

This is a must-have resource for anyone interested in learning how to optimize the SAP CRM Interaction Center. Each chapter describes specific functions in the Interaction Center and why they are useful, and then demonstrates how to use and customize these functions. It covers essential topics, including Computer Telephony Integration and Multi-Channel Integration, IC Service, IC Sales, IC Marketing, and Shared Services Centers. Whether you're new to SAP CRM or a current SAP CRM IC user, this book will provide you with the answers.

approx. 463 pp., 69,95 Euro / US$ 69.95
ISBN 978-1-59229-197-7, Nov 2008

>> www.sap-press.de/1732

Provides a complete guide to preparing for an SAP CRM Implementation from a project-management perspective

Explains how to prepare for integrating the SAP system with existing systems

Includes practical, real-world scenarios for CRM Mobile, Online, and the Interaction Center Web Client

George Fratian

Planning Your SAP CRM Implementation

Written for the CRM implementation team, this book teaches you everything you need to know to prepare for a successful implementation of SAP CRM. Using a hands-on approach with numerous practical examples and scenarios, the book takes you through the key aspects of initiating your plan, including technical design choices, monitoring the project's progress, controlling the scope and why that's important, and how to take your initial project to the next level. This is the one resource you'll need to make your SAP CRM Implementation successful.

276 pp., 2008, 69,95 Euro / US$ 69.95
ISBN 978-1-59229-196-0

>> www.sap-press.de/1735

Gain a holistic understanding of SAP

Make SAP-related decisions with ease

Learn about the SAP landscape, products, solutions, strategies, and more

Nancy Muir, Ian Kimbell

Discover SAP

If you're new to SAP and want to learn more about it, or a decision-maker pressed for time, who needs to gain a holistic understanding of SAP, then this book is for you. A practical, reader-friendly guide for busy professionals, this comprehensive book helps you make quick sense of SAP solutions such as CRM, as well as application integration, SAP NetWeaver and enterprise SOA, embedded analytics, and many other core topics. Plus, learn about SAP as a company, its history, vision, strategies, and much more.

426 pp., 2008, 34,95 Euro / US$ 34.95
ISBN 978-1-59229-117-5

>> www.sap-press.de/1376

Discover what Logistics with SAP is all about and whether its right for your organization

Learn how this powerful, time-tested tool can improve your supply chain and transportation processes to save you money

Martin Murray

Discover Logistics with SAP

With this reader-friendly book, anyone new to SAP or considering implementing it will discover the fundamental capabilities and uses of the Logistics components. You'll learn what's available, and how it works to help you determine if Logistics with SAP is the right tool for your organization. This book is written in a clear, practical style, and uses real-world examples, case studies, and insightful tips to give you a complete overview of the SAP logistics offerings.

approx. 500 pp., 39,95 Euro / US$ 39.95
ISBN 978-1-59229-230-1, Jan 2009

>> www.sap-press.de/1851

Teaches the key business fundamentals and functionality to help make your own processes easier

Provides practical customizing tips and recommendations for your implementation

Includes detailed best-practice examples

Up to date for SAP CRM 2007

Markus Kirchler, Dirk Manhart

Service with SAP CRM

This book will provide a complete guide to SAP CRM 2007 Service, including coverage of functionality, implementation, customization, and Master Data. Readers will get an overview of the functionalities of the service component of SAP CRM 2007, learn how to map them in the SAP system, be introduced to an implementation model, and gather valuable information from two real-life customer examples. The book also deals with the business processes and functionalities of the Service component, so readers will learn about the fast and easy implementation of processes, which do's and don'ts to address, and learn how to ensure the best possible data quality during implementation.

approx. 400 pp., 69,95 Euro / US$ 69.95
ISBN 978-1-59229-206-6, March 2009

>> www.sap-press.de/1773

Interested in reading more?

Please visit our Web site for all
new book releases from SAP PRESS.

www.sap-press.com